Badge #1

Badge #1

True Stories from a Boston Cop

Frankie DeSario

Charleston   London

History
PRESS

Published by The History Press
Charleston, SC 29403
www.historypress.net

Cover images: (top) The author and Gerry Meehan in their TPF squad car, 1965;
(bottom) Joe "Injun Joe" Conforti and the author after an arrest on Somerset Street.

Originally published 2006
The History Press edition 2007

Manufactured in the United Kingdom

ISBN 978.1.59629.293.2

Library of Congress Cataloging-in-Publication Data

DeSario, Frankie.
  Badge #1 : true stories from a Boston cop / Frankie DeSario.
     p. cm.
  ISBN-13: 978-1-59629-293-2 (alk. paper)
  1. DeSario, Frankie. 2. Police--Massachusetts--Boston--Biography. 3. Boston (Mass.). Police
Dept.--History. 4. Police--Massachusetts--Boston--History. I. Title. II. Title: Badge number
one.
  HV7911.D48A3 2007
  363.2092--dc22
  [B]
                              2007024706.

For my wife, Geri, who was always waiting for me, while raising our three kids in our little apartment, never knowing if I would be coming home. She is truly a police officer's wife.

Contents

Foreword

My husband, Frank M. DeSario, has performed many heroic acts during his career as a police officer in Boston. One incident of which I am extremely proud occurred in 1987 when he saved the life of a young baby. I personally wanted to share this with you, the readers of his book. Below find the report of commendation from the Police Department of Boston.

Geri DeSario

Boston Police
August 10, 1987
Recommendation for Commendation
Francis M. DeSario, Police Officer 6063
Special Operation

On Thursday, June 18, 1987, Officer Francis M. DeSario, while off duty, was in the harness shop of the Hughes Horse & Rider Supplies, 15 ʰ Randolph St., Canton, MA.

While inside the shop, Officer DeSario heard what sounded like a muffled thump, then a great deal of commotion followed by hysterical screaming coming from outside the rear of the building. Officer DeSario, along with several other people, rushed outside to find that the ten month-old grandson of the store's owner had fallen down a flight of fifteen stairs, striking his head on the cement landing. The baby had been knocked unconscious and had stopped breathing.

As the family members and other store customers froze in shock and could not help, Officer DeSario immediately rushed to the aid of the infant. Not knowing the extent or seriousness of the baby's injuries, Officer DeSario gently and carefully began CPR and mouth-to-mouth resuscitation. About one and a half minutes later the baby began to breathe.

Still not knowing the extent of the baby's injuries, Officer DeSario gently resisted the family's efforts to take the baby and managed to keep the infant immobile until the ambulance arrived to transport the child to the Goddard Hospital, where it was treated and diagnosed to have suffered a fractured skull.

The doctors at Goddard Hospital, along with the Canton Fire Department Ambulance EMTs Rick Russell and Al Duty, stated that had it not been for Officer DeSario's immediate, capable and caring assistance, they would have certainly lost the baby.

Officer DeSario, the humble and unassuming professional police officer that he is, returned to work the following night, never mentioning the incident to his fellow police officers. Only after we received an emotional and grateful letter from the baby's grandfather did we become aware of this incident and were able to investigate.

Officer DeSario is to be commended for his quick response, his calm and professional handling of an emotional situation, and his humble exit from an incident that, had he not been present, would have certainly resulted in the loss of a helpless baby. This officer is a credit to himself, the Special Operations Division and the Boston Police Department. I therefore strongly recommend that he receive departmental recognition and commendation for his professional action while off duty.

Sgt. Kevin D. Foley, I.D. #6827

A transcript from a fall issue of the Boston Police journal, *Brightlights*, states the following:

Badge #1

Francis M. DeSario, police officer of District A-1, now has the distinguished honor of being the longest serving officer with the Police Department. He was sworn in as a Boston police officer on March 11, 1964. He now has 38 years and more than 8 months as a police officer. The #1 badge was passed down to him by retired fellow district A-1 police officer Jack Bilodeau, who served 39 years, 3 months, and 22 days. Enjoy your retirement, Jack. Francis M. DeSario was appointed to the Boston Police Department on March 11, 1964. He began his career working in the Tactical Patrol Force for almost 10 years. He has had further assignments in the transportation unit, area-B, and finally in district A-1 in 1991, where he will finish his career. Along the way, he has received numerous awards and commendations for meritorious service.

Frank received a commendation in 1977 after he observed a motorcyclist who had crashed into a guard rail and was quickly covered in flames from the leaking fuel tank. Frank attempted to pull the man to safety but was unsuccessful because the cyclist was trapped. Frank then ran to his car, grabbed a blanket, and attempted to cover the man. Once the blanket caught fire, Frank took his own jacket to put out the fire. More EMS personnel arrived and rushed the man to the hospital where he survived. As they took the man to the ambulance Frank was heard saying, "I only wish I could have done more for the poor guy."

Frank finally wears the #1 badge as our district A-1 motorcycle officer assigned to a downtown crossing and the North End. Keep up the good work Frank.

Acknowledgements

To a friend I have never met but without whose help this book would not have been possible. Shelly Rosenberg, thank you.

To Judy Sparrow Carroll who found Shelly for me.

To my beautiful children Patty, Frankie Jr. and Lisa who sacrificed by my long hours of work; my grandchildren Stephen, Lisa, Mark, Paige, Michael, Frankie and Maria; my marine brother Mike and special thoughts of my wonderful sister Angela who passed away

To the Boston Police Department, Special Operations and my beloved Tactical Patrol Force.

Patrolling Quincy Market.

1.

Beginning of the Ride

Sitting in front of my computer, I'm trying to work up enough courage to do something that I've wanted to do since my retirement in June of 2003 after thirty-nine years and three months of service with the Boston Police Department. As I look back on my career, I can't help but think how much I want to share my experiences with others.

When I was nineteen years old, I didn't have a care in the world. I lived at home with Mom, Dad and my two kid sisters. I was driving a truck, making a few bucks and had been dating a beautiful blonde named Geri for two years. My big brother Mike (my idol) had just gotten married after being discharged from the U.S. Marines. He urged me to try to land a job with the local police department.

When Mike spoke, I listened. I enrolled in Matt Connolly's Civil Service School for a six-month course and passed the test upon completion. I was then put on the Police Academy's waiting list.

It was 1961 and things were starting to heat up in Southeast Asia. Rumors of the Selective Service were circulating and I knew I would be going into the military. But I didn't want to lose the girl of my dreams—I knew she was the girl I was going to marry from the first day that I met her. I wasn't going to take any chances, so off we went to pick out an engagement ring and I asked Geri to be my wife. I joined the U.S. Army Reserves and began my six months' active duty and six and a half years in the reserves. I was discharged in February 1962 and Geri and I were married on April 21, 1963.

After my term of service, I went back to work driving a truck and wondering if the police department had forgotten about me. They had not. On March 11, 1964, I began what would be the most exciting and, on occasion, the most unrewarding job a person could have.

2.

Rookie Days

How Proud I Was

There I was, a pretty tough kid from the Roxbury-Dorchester area of Boston, starting to realize that staying out of trouble as a kid really paid off. Thanks to the training I received from the Sisters of Charity (Halifax) at St. Patrick's Grammar School, my experiences at Holy Cross Cathedral High School in the South End of Boston and the important influence of my family—the iron fists of my dad, my brother Mike and the guidance of the "boss of bosses," my mom—I felt big and bad and ready for anything!

I was sworn in at 10:00 a.m. on a cold, gloomy Wednesday morning, March 11, 1964, by Deputy Superintendent Taylor at Boston Police Headquarters on Berkley Street. I was addressed and welcomed by Commissioner Edmund McNamara and was later assigned to the training unit of the Boston Police Academy at 7 Warren Avenue. I still couldn't believe all of this was really happening. I'll never forget being issued a winter uniform coat and a hat with badge #1315. We were greeted by Deputy Superintendent Cadigan at 1:00 p.m. and were then issued our lecture materials and other equipment by Lieutenant Burke. Finally, Sergeant Barney Schroeder gave us the academy rules.

I'll never forget how proud I was that day.

Reality

The activities at the academy were mostly routine. We learned about the evolution of the Boston Police Department and its critical areas. My class consisted of forty-five young, eager men who could hardly wait to hit the street. Time in the academy seemed to drag, but it was apparent that this training was essential in order to become a good officer.

On March 18, 1964, we received our revolvers, Colt .38s, and began learning their proper use and care. After three weeks at the range we were ready to head to the streets with the veterans for some on-the-job training.

One night, alone and away from my class, I walked into Station 10 at Roxbury Crossing, one of the toughest precincts in the city, to begin my first tour of duty in a cruiser. I wore a pair of winter pants and a new starched shirt and was proud to display my shiny new badge. I also had my Colt revolver and six-inch service baton. I'll always remember the 11:45 p.m. roll call, standing and hearing my name called along with veteran Officer John Carozza and the look on his face when he learned I was assigned to him: Oh shit, why me?

Heading to the cruiser, he said, "Hey kid, we're the 10A car. Get in and don't touch the radio."

Just around midnight, Carozza spotted a stolen car in motion on Hammond Street and told me to start up the siren. In those days, the siren was located on the roof of the cruiser and connected to a small button on the dashboard. Not knowing that you were supposed to hit the button intermittently, I held it down as we chased the stolen car through the streets of Roxbury. The siren burned out and the awful smell of smoldering wire filled the car.

Meanwhile, the two car thieves jumped out of the "hotbox" and ran in opposite directions. I chased my suspect into an alley surrounded by tenement houses and spotted him by a dumpster. He was holding a knife.

"This can't be," I thought to myself. "Not on my first night on the job."

As I pulled out my service revolver the suspect bolted into the night. At that exact moment Carozza appeared. "Put away your gun! It's only a stolen car!" he shouted, unaware that the suspect had a knife.

I'll never forget going back to the station, my mouth as dry as the Sahara Desert, sweat pouring down my face as Carozza complained to the others about getting stuck with the rookie who'd pulled out a gun on a stolen car suspect. He demanded never to be stuck with a rookie again.

I felt like the loneliest cop in the world.

BLOOD AND GUTS

Talking amongst ourselves about our first assignments, my classmates and I learned that none of the veterans wanted to work with a rookie, especially the older ones. The old-timers felt that we were cutting into their territory and had interrupted their routine. Every rookie had his horror stories to tell but we all agreed to do our best to get the veterans to accept us. All rookies were treated the same way.

As we headed upstairs at Station 2 at Milk Street, we held our breath in anticipation of our new on-the-job training assignments. As it turned out, I got a great one tagging cars on Commonwealth Avenue.

From May 12 to June 11, 1964, I walked a beat in the North End on Richmond to North Streets. Everything was going well—just an occasional drunk arrest, some traffic arguments, nothing I couldn't handle—and I was getting a little cocky.

But things soon changed. At 8:45 a.m., while I was tagging on Prince Street, I observed two men fighting. Both were going at it at a good clip. One of the men, "Red" Scalafanti, turned on me unexpectedly with a broom handle and struck me on the top of my head. I started to bleed profusely down my face and all over my white shirt. I remember looking up at him like he was a Roman gladiator. I was in good shape, too, and I'm sure he later wished he had never met me. "Red" wanted to continue fighting and, after a further struggle, I was able to subdue and arrest him until help arrived.

While all of this was going on somebody put in a call that a rookie cop was in trouble in North Square and he was bleeding. Cars and wagons started coming from every direction. All three of us were taken to the hospital where I was treated for minor injuries: a laceration of the scalp and scraped knuckles. Later, "Red" Scalafanti was arrested and booked at District 1 for assault and battery with a dangerous weapon.

It is customary for the defendant to be arraigned the following morning at the Boston Municipal Court and I, as the complainant, would seek a grievance against him if I thought it necessary. On Tuesday, June 2, 1964, I was ordered to appear in municipal court for alleged assault.

This was my first appearance in a courtroom acting as the complainant as the arresting officer, so naturally I was unfamiliar with the surroundings and the procedure for applying for a complaint. I was approached by the detective who worked in the court. He informed me that the man I arrested just lost his temper and never intended to hurt me. Furthermore, he was a community leader and wanted to apologize to me, which he did. At the time I had no idea that the detective who worked in the court was a Boston police officer assigned to the court. I was relieved to avoid the courtroom and took some satisfaction in knowing that Mr. Scalafanti would always remember me since he fared much worse in the altercation.

About a year went by and I was getting more familiar with court procedure as well as getting to know more of my brother officers. We always helped each other out in every way possible by backing each other up and by prosecuting those who would try to hurt us. So when I found out that the detective was a police officer assigned to the court I became quite bitter. I couldn't believe a fellow cop wouldn't prosecute to the full extent of the law. In his mind, he thought he had done the right thing by helping a community leader. I later had a long conversation with the detective and expressed my disdain for his actions. He said he was sorry but that he felt he had done the right thing.

First Assignment

On July 10, 1964, I graduated from the academy on Legion Highway and was assigned to District 13, Jamaica Plain, making a salary of $108 per week. A few days out of the academy I felt I'd earned my right to be there. Something I'd learned in those short months: always be alert and always use your head. Now I could relate to St. Patrick's Grammar School where every classroom you entered had a sign above the door that read: THINK. Working Jamaica Plain could get boring as it wasn't considered a busy "house," but every now and then something would happen to keep things interesting.

On July 20, 1964, I was working the morning watch with a guy named "Red" Walsh. "Red" was a former marine who had somehow fought at Iwo Jima when he was only seventeen. This guy had more guts than anyone I had ever met. Most of the time, during the morning watch (essentially the middle of the night), police "dig in," which means an officer might pick a favorite spot, park and hang out there waiting for something to happen. But not "Red." He was always out looking for the bad guys.

At 3:05 a.m. "Red" spotted a Chevy convertible whose occupant was wanted for indecent assault and battery and a supermarket hold-up in Jamaica Plain. I remember three of the men were hiding in the car behind the supermarket and "Red" reached in and grabbed one of the occupants whose nickname was "Kid Boston." "Kid" was wanted for indecent assault and battery and maiming (biting the nipple of a breast off a young girl). The other two men ran in the direction of the grounds of a Catholic convent.

"Red" and I checked the unlit grounds and then, as if by total instinct, "Red" aimed his flashlight at the corner of the field while drawing his service revolver. The beam of his flashlight caught a man crouched down, pointing a gun in our direction. I think I froze, but "Red" jumped on him and confiscated his gun. All this occurred with no other cars available. "What a cop!" I thought.

William "Red" Walsh showed me how to approach criminals in the act and how to react properly. That was a first felony arrest that no rookie could ever forget. The way he approached the suspects—outnumbered and with a rookie partner—took a lot of guts, especially since I virtually froze while "Red" possibly saved my life.

I knew I would never forget "Red" Walsh.

3.

Enter Tactical Patrol Force

PERFECT PARTNERS

At this time, with the Vietnam War escalating, things started to heat up in Boston. Protests were beginning and crowds made up mostly of students were starting to get out of control. The city had to do something to keep the peace.

In 1962, under the direction of Commissioner Edmund McNamara, the Tactical Patrol Force (TPF) was created. It initially consisted of a few detectives and a handful of men under the leadership of Captain John Hanlon, the first commander. As time went by the size of the unit had to be increased. In July of 1964 headquarters started recruiting new members.

Before joining the TPF we were taught how essential it is to work and think together and particularly how crucial it is for partners to know what the other is thinking. Ingrained in my memory from a few months earlier in the Police Academy is a phrase the instructors were always trying to impress on us: try to think as one. As part of our training—getting away from learning the basics such as right of arrest, various types of crimes, etc—the instructors used different antics to see what one recruit thought and then to observe what another thought or saw.

Such was the case one particular day in the academy when I first met Gerry Meehan. During one class the instructor flashed onto a movie screen different obscure objects for a quick second and then asked the class of forty-four to try to identify the object and write down what we saw. It seemed that no two recruits saw the same object, so as we all laughed and joked the instructor turned to me and asked what I saw. I told him the object

At TPF headquarters; me, Ken Hegner and Gerry Meehan.

looked to me like a piece of lasagna. With that Gerry Meehan jumped up with his piece of paper and exclaimed that he saw the same thing. Jokingly, I said to Gerry that we were destined to be partners. But Gerry was sent to one precinct and I to another and we didn't see each other again until we were both interviewed for the TPF.

On Wednesday, July 29, 1964, I was interviewed by Deputy Superintendent Howland to become a member of the TPF. I was accepted and on Monday, August 3, 1964, I reported to the Police Academy to begin duty with the TPF. From the very first day through the completion of our training on August 15, we received extensive instruction in special weapons, shotguns, pistols and riot control formations. We watched numerous films on riot control and were taught physical exercises by Officer Jon Dorr of the Boston Police Department and State Police Lieutenant Owens.

Gerry and I finished our TPF training and because we got along so well and seemed to think alike, we asked the captain if we could be partners. Gerry was a big strong army veteran, an ex-paratrooper in the 82nd Airborne, who was born and raised in the Bronx. There was no denying his birthplace and I would often joke about his New York tongue. Gerry and I ran up a pretty good arrest record and we became great partners. Gerry had no driver's license so I was the designated driver and Gerry always said I was a good wheelman. We would often brag about how we never lost a stolen car in a chase and we always got our man. Gerry could run like a deer so whenever a suspect jumped out of a stolen car he would chase him on foot and run him down—and he never failed to let me know how fast he was.

One night I'll never forget we chased a stolen car with suspects wanted for other crimes as well. I drove through the streets of Roxbury where I grew up, knowing every street and alley in the area like the back of my hand. The stolen car couldn't shake us so the two suspects in the car decided to bolt and they ran from the car. The man in the passenger side fled on foot with Gerry in hot pursuit. Gerry chased him for what seemed like forever. He got his man and started walking back to the cruiser never expecting me to have caught my man. As luck would have it, after my man started to run he was apprehended by other officers who were assisting and they handed him over to me less than twenty feet from the cruiser. So there I was, relaxed and waiting for Gerry to come back. When he arrived huffing and puffing and saw me sitting there, I said to him, "What took you so long? I chased my man for over a hundred yards."

That was a night to remember.

Me and Gerry Meehan in our TPF squad car, 1965.

RIOT IN THE SQUARE

When we started, the TPF had three cruisers and most of the surveillance of the city was done on foot. This foot unit saturated the city's hotspots, walking two abreast from the Combat Zone to Codman Square in Dorchester. Sometimes we worked as decoys, dressed as old ladies or homeless people, and sometimes we drove taxis trying to root out those who committed serious crimes. No matter what we were involved in, however, we were brought together at a moment's notice for crowd control.

I remember vividly patrolling the Park Square area one night and then being picked up by a bus along with other members of the TPF. While on the bus, we were informed that there was big trouble in the Harvard Square area and that it had been overrun. All the way there we sang "God Bless America." As the bus came to a stop it was pelted with bricks. On the bus with us, with the hopes of giving us spiritual guidance, was one of the bravest Catholic priests I have ever met. His name was Father Jim Lane, chaplain of the Boston Police Department. When we got off the bus I can remember more than one man offering the chaplain his service baton, which he promptly refused.

When the bus doors opened, we could not believe what was going on. The town was literally being burned to the ground. Upon exiting the bus and falling into riot formation Lieutenant Bill McDonald, "Mr. TPF," gave the order to "move them out." We were able to clear the area so that the fire department could enter Harvard Square. There we were, forty tactical officers, mostly ex-servicemen, all in the six-foot tall range, wearing our new jumpsuits, black boots and helmets and armed with our new three-foot batons.

TPF officers at work at the Northeastern riot.

I remember not being able to get into the proper riot formation because of the debris being thrown at us. The TPF usually formed groups of five officers along a line to move as one. The situation at Harvard Square was so out of control that we couldn't get into the standard formation and had to move through the crowd as one unit.

The rioters at Harvard Square were intent on burning down buildings, vandalizing property and hurting the police officers trying to protect the property in the process. Firefighters were being pelted with bricks as they responded to fires in the square. Many rioters threw Molotov cocktails— gasoline in a bottle—at the police and private property while some waved Viet Cong flags.

Unfortunately there were those who condemned our actions, saying the TPF acted too aggressively. The rioters themselves issued complaints; I suspect because they were furious that the TPF prevented them from being successful in their mission. The TPF itself always maintained a positive point of view in any situation in which it was involved.

Eventually the rioting stopped and partial peace was restored.

Back at the bus, we were stopped by the town manager, a man named Mr. Sullivan. He proceeded to walk beside the bus, scratching his head and stopping to say, "Thank you," and "God Bless the TPF! Without you we would have lost Harvard Square."

We returned to TPF headquarters for a critique session. Whenever the TPF was used as a unit, whether for a riot situation or a hostage situation, there always followed a critique session. All the officers, along with the squad leaders and commanders, would gather together to rehash that particular incident and question whether changes needed to be made to improve TPF action in future situations.

Later that week headquarters began receiving mail commending the tactics of the Boston Police Department and inquiring about the TPF. Word quickly spread about how fast and disciplined the TPF was and soon we were being requested to patrol other parts of the city. It was such an honor to be a member and to wear the Tactical Patrol Force patch on our upper right arms. The unit had gained much respect because of our actions in Harvard Square.

The TPF was there for riots in Roxbury, countless anti-war protests and in South Boston in 1974 to protect the children, both black and white, during the start of forced busing. Again and again we were called in to manage situations and we always did an outstanding job. Many books have been written about the TPF and how it was both necessary and aggressive.

4.

Vice Control Unit

Sitting back in my recliner today and reading my diary from the early days of the TPF, I can't forget my partner Gerry Meehan. Because we worked so well together, we were picked to work undercover in the Vice Control Unit. Our main objective was to look out for booking activity and prostitution and to field interrogation reports on suspicious persons in the North Station area.

That assignment began on February 25, a cold and windy day. Undercover, we'd sit in bars such as Landmark Café, the Four Winds and Mario's Deli, sipping beer—always draught since the department was paying for it. Some of the time we looked grubby because we were "made." Being "made" means working undercover. Say you're in disguise and in hostile territory and someone in the crowd spots you and knows that you're a cop; you'd tell your colleagues, "That person made me."

We continued that assignment until March 6, spending on the average four dollars a day, as neither Gerry nor I were big drinkers. I remember at the end of the week, after working the North End, walking into Lieutenant Paul Russell's office hoping to get reimbursed and trying to look completely sober. But Lieutenant Paul Russell always gave us a look that made us feel guilty. Without a doubt Lieutenant Russell, later to become Superintendent Russell, was the smartest boss I ever worked for.

Gerry and I were next assigned to go undercover driving taxis, as there had been a rash of holdups in the city and the cabbies needed protection. We had several near busts but nothing panned out.

One night, after driving around for hours, we "dug in" at a secluded area in the Washington Park section of Roxbury, the high crime area of Boston. What a mistake that turned out to be. Before we knew it, we were

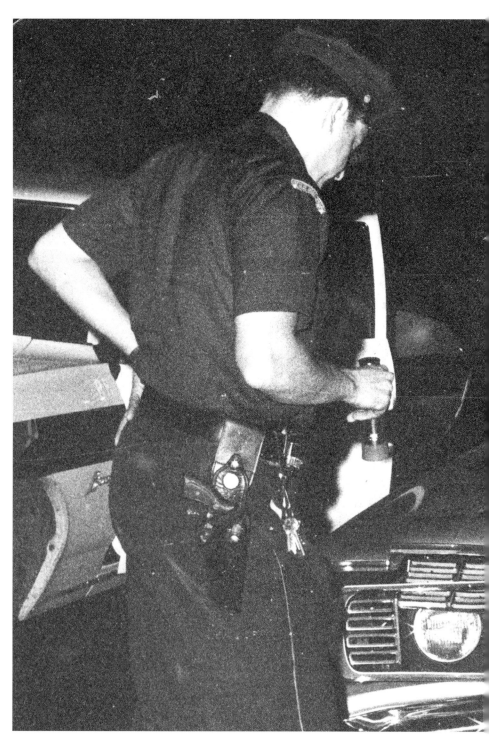

Me and Gerry—all in a day's work.

Gerry tagging downtown.

surrounded by at least ten Boston cruisers, our brothers, with their guns drawn, also trying to nab suspects holding up cabbies. They proceeded to drag us out of the cab and threw us to the ground, in spite of the fact that we kept yelling "We're cops! We're cops!" It was no fun looking down the barrels of so many revolvers.

The Vice Control Unit also had teams decoyed as street people in the hopes of nabbing muggers in the downtown area. We worked in teams of three. One officer acted as if he were drunk and had his wallet hanging out of his right rear pocket. The idea was that if the suspected mugger tried to rob him, the other two officers would move in and make an arrest. The "victim" would drop a white handkerchief to alert the team that he was getting robbed.

Most of the time it was slow with only an occasional arrest, but there was one night I'll never forget. We set up our team in front of the old Hillbilly Ranch in the Park Square area and on this particular night I was to play the drunk. Things had been quiet and I guess my team wasn't alert. I acted the part with my wallet sticking out as I leaned against the Ranch, when all of a sudden a mugger approached me with a knife. I dropped my hanky, but my team was distracted by something else and didn't notice I was being robbed. Struggling with the suspect, I managed to retrieve my service revolver and arrest him on my own. Needless to say I was furious. After that, we had a meeting and agreed to never let down our guard when working that operation. From that point on, we were very successful and made several good arrests.

Gerry and I were on a roll. When we weren't working undercover, we'd be together in a cruiser, either in the Combat Zone or in Roxbury making some good arrests. We were given two days off for every felony arrest and one for any misdemeanor arrest. I remember Gerry and I playing the Magnolia Street area, a dumping ground for stolen cars and an area very familiar to me, as it was where I grew up. In a very short time Gerry and I accumulated over twenty-eight days off. As a team, Gerry and I worked well.

5.

DA's Office, Homicide

After working on the street with the TPF for a couple of years, I entered the most thrilling, exciting and dangerous time of my career. On June 6, 1966, I was assigned to the District Attorney's Office, Homicide Squad. How proud I was! There I was, not quite twenty-seven years old and working with the "detective of detectives," District Attorney Garrett Byrne.

Things were heating up in the turf war for control of illegal activities in Boston—in Charlestown, Somerville and Roxbury. Bodies were popping up all over the city. There was Connie Hughes from Charlestown, shot while driving in Revere. Buddy McLean from Somerville was gunned down on Broadway in his hometown. The Bennett Brothers from Dorchester were missing. Rumor had it that more killings were planned. District Attorney Byrne was so concerned that he created a task force whose sole duty was to investigate gangland murders and to put a stop to them.

Byrne selected a fearless veteran investigator, Lieutenant Salvatore Ingenere, to lead the task force. Ingenere patrolled the streets of Roxbury and later the Fields Corner section of Dorchester. "Old Sal" rose quickly through the ranks and was promoted to sergeant detective early in his career.

On the street Lieutenant Sal had lots of contacts. He knew every bookie, loan shark and good thief in the Roxbury-Dorchester area. In fact, they were the source of his information. They knew that if Sal didn't get what he wanted it would mean serious trouble for them.

Sal trusted no one, yet he had to pick a squad. He recruited Detective Joe McCain and Detective Leo Papille from the Metropolitan District Commission (MDC) Police. Then he took his old friend from his days in Dorchester, Arthur Cardarelli. He brought in John Enright, Donald

McGowan and a cop from the North End recruited out of the TPF, "Injun Joe" Conforti, who was also a former lightweight contender. And then there was me, the runt of the litter.

I met Sal when I was a teenager and he was walking the Fields Corner beat. I used to play pinball at the Lucky Strike Bowling Alleys, especially the machines that "paid off." Officer Ingenere often warned me to stay away from the pinball machines, especially the ones that paid out because you had to be over eighteen and I wasn't. One night, when I had a lot of money invested in the machine, Officer Ingenere walked over to me and told me to "screw." I told him that I would in a minute. Big mistake. He grabbed me by my shoulder and threw me out the door.

As I got older I wised up and learned to respect the law and especially Officer Sal. Eventually we became friends. He remembered me when I joined the Boston Police and, because I had a good record with the TPF, he recruited me.

Looking back, we were pretty much aware of most of the goings-on throughout the city, but we didn't know about what was happening in South Boston. Sure, we knew that Whitey Bulger was the kingpin of all illegal activity in that area. We also knew that he was friendly with many law enforcement officers and he was considered by some to be a sort of Robin Hood in Southie. We also knew of his relationship with Stephen Flemmi and that they controlled the gambling and loan-sharking operations in the Dorchester area. What we didn't know was that they were being protected by the FBI, the State Police and even the Boston Police.

These guys essentially did what they pleased. I remember locating a garage in Roxbury where cars belonging to hit men were being stored, including a gold Oldsmobile owned by Joseph "the Animal" Barboza. I thought I had hit the lottery. But as I was leaving the garage, a Boston detective who identified himself as being "from Intelligence" asked me what I found. When I told him, he asked that I not report it and I agreed. The next day, the cars were gone.

Looking back I consider myself lucky for getting out of that outfit in less than two years. There we were, the DA's own task force, out every night hunting the bad guys, only to learn that they'd been tipped off.

6.

Meet "the Animal"

The Beach Ball

Joseph "the Animal" Barboza, originally from the Fall River-New Bedford area, had once been a professional boxer who fell in with the local mafia and became a leg breaker and enforcer. When he saw how much cash was flowing into the operation, he decided he wasn't getting a big enough slice of the pie. Along with his faithful companion Joseph "Chico" D'Amico, he walked into the Peppermint Lounge on Stuart Street in Boston, which was owned and operated by Peter Fiumara, a soldier in the local mafia. Barboza approached Fiumara and announced that he was Fiumara's new partner. Recognizing Barboza, Fiumara told Barboza to "get the fuck out." With that, "Chico" cut Fiumara's throat from ear to ear.

When members of the task force visited Fiumara at the hospital, he refused to name his assailant, even after hours of questioning. However, word spread quickly of a $50,000 contract on Joe Barboza. Unfazed, Barboza continued on his murderous ways, with several bodies popping up in the greater Boston area.

One of Barboza's favorite hangouts was the Beach Ball Bar on the strip along Revere Beach, a joint where just about all the hoods and "wanna-be" hoods hung out. This was Barboza's favorite joint. Along with "the Animal" and "Chico" there would be Guy Frizzi, Nicky Femia and occasionally Arthur "Tash" Bratsos, who idolized Barboza. This group ruled the Beach Ball and Lieutenant Ingenere always made it a point for us to drop-in, especially on weekends.

Detective Joe McCain, before coming to the task force, had been assigned to MDC headquarters and had a confrontation with Joe "the Animal" at the Beach Ball a few years earlier. McCain was attempting to bring Barboza in and Barboza threatened him, saying he was only brave because he had a badge and a gun. With that, McCain invited Barboza down to the Revere Beach boardwalk. He'd done some fighting in the U.S. Navy and had also been a heavyweight contender. McCain flattened Barboza, so you can imagine how much he hated the detective. To find out later that McCain was a member of the task force only infuriated Barboza more. McCain had as much disdain for Barboza as Barboza did for him. One night in Revere Beach they casually bumped into each other. As Barboza threw a punch, McCain knocked Barboza to the beach. McCain was afraid of no one.

On the night of July 24, 1966, at the Beach Ball, a kid from Dorchester was flirting with the girls at the club and doing well for himself. His name was Arthur Pearson, a tall, maybe six-foot four, 200 pound Adonis, who was dancing and having a ball with Barboza and "Chico's" girls. Arthur was making his moves when at the same moment "Chico" and "the Animal" made theirs. Barboza and "Chico" allegedly sliced Pearson from his belly button down to his crotch. He began bleeding profusely. The kid from Dorchester almost died that night, but because he was so strong and healthy up until that point he managed to survive.

During his stay at a Boston hospital, friends and family came to visit Arthur and I'm sure they told him what a mistake he had made. I remember walking into his hospital room along with Lieutenant Ingenere and observing Arthur lying there in bed, tubes running out of his nose, wires coming out of his genital area, an intravenous in his left arm and bandages covering his nose and cheekbones. I stood at the foot of the bed listening and watching as Lieutenant Ingenere interviewed him. It seemed that he had gotten the message from Barboza and "Chico" and he refused to talk, even though Sal threatened him for being a hostile witness.

The task force continued searching and hoping to get more tips as to what Barboza might be planning. Up to this point none of us would dare to admit—or were crazy enough to think—that Whitey Bulger and Stevie "the Rifleman" Flemmi, with the help of the FBI's H. Paul Rico, could successfully lure Barboza away from being a hit man for the Angiullo brothers. Bulger, Flemmi and Barboza—what a dream team! Meanwhile, one of their closest associates, Johnny Martaranno, still unaware that his partners were rats, kept doing his thing at the request of Bulger and Flemmi. Things were going so smoothly for them that they had free reign to do anything they wanted, including murder.

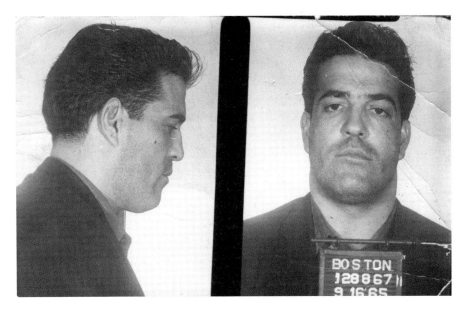

Joe "the Animal" Barboza.

Habitual Criminal

Ingenere was no fool. He had always been a bookworm and knew the law regarding the right of arrest. Suddenly we had a warrant for Joe Barboza's arrest. Because Barboza had committed many crimes and violated parole, we were able to charge him with "being a habitual criminal." That helped us get Barboza off the street, at least for a little while, and let him know we were alive and well.

On a fall morning in 1966 the lieutenant and other members of the task force were already in the office, and were joined by two other detectives from homicide, Detectives Cunningham and Nee, two of Boston's best. There they were loading their revolvers, checking their ammo, loading a shotgun and preparing to go out and get Joe Barboza. With Barboza's notorious temper no one was taking any chances.

As they were planning their strategy and putting their guns in their holsters, Sal told me to "stay and answer the phone." I felt truly betrayed. After all the nights I had driven around going out of my mind looking for Barboza, I couldn't believe I was being left behind to kill time by going through files of past Boston murders and waiting for the phone to ring. Then my door opened.

I rolled in my chair toward the door to see who had entered. There I was, the youngest, most inexperienced member of the task force, alone in

41

Stevie "the Rifleman" Flemmi.

the office, with Al Farrese, an attorney, standing at my door with his client, none other than Joe Barboza, in tow. Farrese told me that they were aware of the warrant for Barboza's arrest and that he had advised Barboza to turn himself in. As I looked up, I came face to face with the ugliest, scariest individual I had ever seen.

The best detectives in the city were out looking for this ferocious killer. They were well-armed. Meanwhile, there I was, sitting behind a typewriter with a small, five-shot Banker's Special by my side, booking Joe Barboza.

Once I filled out the report, I handcuffed "the Animal" and led him to the prisoners' elevator for the ride down to City Prison where Barboza was searched and put into a cell.

Back in my office, I wiped the sweat off my brow and wondered what had just happened. Had I done the right thing? Should I have called for assistance? Was the lieutenant going to be angry because I didn't attempt to call him?

Several hours later, the task force returned looking frustrated and tired. They walked by me as I tried to get someone's attention. I finally caught up to the lieutenant and I started mumbling about how I got Barboza downstairs in the city lockup.

He looked at me in amazement. "Are you kidding?" he asked. Sal asked the sergeant at the desk for the booking sheet and checked if I had indeed just booked Joe Barboza.

A smile crept slowly across his face.

I'll never forget that once Barboza made bail, I watched Sal's face as he noticed something in Barboza's hand as he headed out the door: a pad of paper with the names of the officers on the task force. From that day on, one of my tasks became to pick up the boss every morning and drive him to our office.

One morning, on the way to our office Sal said, "Go to headquarters and sign out for a shotgun and ammo." Later I asked him why. He told me he was concerned for the safety of his men and for himself. Every morning I would have the shotgun with me when I picked him up and in the evening I'd escort him to his front door with the gun in hand.

7.

Domestic Affairs

As time went on, the secrecy of the other squad on the sixth floor was getting more and more frustrating. Our task force was specifically assigned to gangland murders and the detectives across the hall were supposed to be handling "domestic affairs," which meant all serious crimes *except* gangland murders. Yet, when there was a hit, there they were, even though we would get the call. We never knew why. Nor did we know why we were told not to talk to them. It seemed we would be out all day and night futilely visiting bars, nightclubs and hangouts throughout Suffolk County (Revere and Swampscott) where we knew Barboza once lived, near the home of his buddy "Chico" D'Amico and around East Boston, as well as the bars along Bennington Street. I was much too inexperienced to know the reason for all of the secrecy then.

The Domestic Affairs unit was led by Commander John Doyle, who, as a patrolman, directed traffic on the corner of Beacon and Charles Streets at the foot of the courthouse. Every morning, the DA's car with Garret Byrne inside would pass by Officer Doyle and they became friends. John Doyle was assigned to the DA's office, Domestic Affairs, with the brand new title of commander, heading all of the men we weren't supposed to associate with. Commander Doyle, a man who had never taken a promotional exam in his career, all of a sudden became a superintendent from his civil service rank of patrolman.

Knowing what I now know, it seems Domestic Affairs had more protection than we had and I wonder what Agent Rico and the FBI would have done if one of us got killed. We started to see that not only were we playing a losing game, but we weren't making any money at it and many of us started to think about leaving. Because our morale was low and we took out our frustration by constantly complaining and arguing with each other, things started to fall apart from within.

One night, just after I had lost my grandmother, the boss called me to pick him up to go "cruising." I explained my circumstances and told him I didn't feel like going out. He raised his voice at me then hung up the phone. The next day he called me into his office and started to lay into me for not going out. I told him that my family came first and he yelled at me and called me a punk. I lunged at him, putting him against the wall.

I have to remind myself that we didn't know then what we know now, even though we were always suspicious. Barboza and company knew who they had on their side, but we didn't. Meanwhile the wiseguys were having meetings right under our noses at locations right there in the North End. Attending these meetings were law enforcement people, "friends" of Whitey Bulger and Stevie Flemmi. Those guys must have felt comfortable knowing they had so many high-ranking officers in their pocket.

8.

Gangland Heats Up

"RALPHIE CHONG" LAMATTINA

Ingenere brought in two top-notch detectives, Dennis Casey and Arthur Linsky, to help in our endeavor to get Joe Barboza permanently off the street. Casey and Linsky had information they had picked up from their stoolies during their days in Vice and Narcotics. They received information that "the Animal" was about to make another hit somewhere near a bar in the downtown Boston area. The target was an ex-con who had been singing to the Feds. On October 6, 1966, Casey and Linsky stopped Barboza's car on Washington Street near Congress Street. A search of the car turned up an M1 rifle with a loaded clip inside, plus several rounds of ammo, along with other weapons.

Finally we had Barboza behind bars on a decent rap. At his arraignment his bail was set at over $125,000 cash. That made a lot of us happy. Who would dare come forward and post that kind of money for a guy that hot who was hated by the local mafia guys?

Apparently "the Animal" did have at least two more friends: Arthur "Tash" Bratsos and Thomas DiPriscio, an ex-boxer from the Roslindale section of Boston who had been an enforcer for local loan sharks. They admired Barboza and wanted to be just like him and they vowed to "the Animal" that they would find the money to bail him out. What a mistake.

Apparently they had forgotten that their hero was a hated man in the North End when they foolishly headed to a local mafia-owned lounge, the Nite Lite, and told the local hoods that they were raising money for their buddy, Joe Barboza, and that they were $85,000 short.

This infuriated the patrons of the club, especially Ralph "Ralphie Chong" LaMattina, a soldier in the local mafia. Word had it that Ralphie jumped to his feet, drew an automatic and started spraying the two with bullets while yelling all kinds of obscenities.

Behind the bar was a small hallway and a door that led to a narrow alleyway to Commercial Street. Parked there was a 1964 gray Cadillac sedan, registered to Arthur Bratsos of Doone Street in Medford, who happened to live right across the street from one of the Angiullo brothers. Ralphie and some of the other patrons managed to get the bodies out of the club and into the back seat of the sedan.

The next morning, November 15, 1966, a cruiser patrolling the A Street area of South Boston was flagged down by a citizen who claimed there were two men "sleeping" in the back seat of a Cadillac. Well, there they were, one on top of the other on the floor in the rear of Bratsos's car.

Word quickly spread about what had happened and the North End was crawling with cops. The men of the task force, along with Lieutenant Ingenere, investigated the club and saw that the rugs had been removed and the mirrors shattered. No one was coming forward with any information. To our surprise, Domestic Affairs was on the scene to "assist in the investigation."

The North End was so hot it completely shut down the normal daily routine of booking and loan-sharking. Ralphie fell out of favor with his own people. Knowing he was going to be punished by the "local businessmen," Ralphie willingly turned himself in.

He, along with his attorney, Jimmy "Little Flower" Morrelli, appeared before Judge Tauro. The judge asked Morrelli to enter a plea. Morrelli replied "not guilty" at the same time as Ralphie answered "guilty." Morrelli looked at Ralphie in amazement and was nudged by Ralphie to be quiet. Ralphie knew he'd be safer in jail and he gladly accepted the charge of being an accessory to murder.

Meanwhile, Barboza, trying to make a deal, sang like a bird about the operations in the North End. It worked. He gave the Feds what they wanted and the Feds gave him what he wanted—a license to go out and kill again, which he did. Gang-related hits in the Boston area continued and it seemed that every time we got a good lead the bad guys would get tipped off. The lieutenant started to become more and more concerned and kept telling us to be alert.

At the time, I wouldn't let myself believe that corrupt deals were being made right under our noses and that the information Barboza gave the Feds was all lies that sent innocent people to jail while he was set free. I can only imagine how loud he laughed as he strolled out of the courtroom.

HIT ON "CHICO"

On December 8, 1966, our office got a call that "Chico," Barboza's faithful friend and ally, was about to be clipped. With information from other departments and calls by some of the undercover cops, we knew where to find him.

Ingenere, along with Detectives Cardarelli, Papille and myself, jumped into our unmarked 1964 stick shift cruiser and headed for Squires restaurant in Revere. When we pulled into the parking lot of the swinging joint on the outskirts of Boston, Ingenere ordered Cardarelli and me to enter the establishment to see if "Chico" was sitting at his usual table at the end of the bar. Walking in with Cardarelli, my heart was pumping a mile a minute as we got patted down more than twice on our way to D'Amico's table.

I knew "Chico" because of his many appearances in municipal court and he had always felt comfortable talking to me. He was far from being an angel, however, with many arrests and convictions for assault and battery with a dangerous weapon and he was very good with a knife. Also at his table were Guy Frizzi and James "Jimmy" Kearns, two notorious hit men who gave us hateful looks.

I told "Chico" that there was a threat out on his life and that we could help him. During this conversation my legs were shaking so much I couldn't control them. "Chico" asked us if we wanted a drink, which I gladly accepted. I told him that Lieutenant Ingenere was in the parking lot and wanted to talk to him. "Chico" stood up, thanked us and told us he already knew about the contract, but to thank the lieutenant anyway. I said goodbye to "Chico," gulped down my V.O. and water and started to leave.

Back in the parking lot, we told Sal what had just taken place and he told us to stay in our car and to be ready to roll. Shortly thereafter, "Chico" and Kearns left the club and got into a green sedan, with Kearns at the wheel. They sped off on Route 1 toward Boston.

As they pulled out of the parking lot, a black sedan parked on the other side of the highway took off after them. We followed, but it was nearly impossible to keep up with them. When we finally caught up at the exit ramp, we found "Chico's" car wrapped around a tree, steam coming from the engine. Sal jumped out of our car and ran to the driver's side to get Kearns. I headed to the passenger's side to get "Chico," but when I opened the car door, "Chico" fell into the street, his forehead blown off.

Kearns, his left cheekbone grazed by a bullet, was smiling, which infuriated Sal. All of a sudden Sal ordered us to arrest Kearns.

"What am I being arrested for?" Kearns demanded.

"Accessory before and after," Sal replied. He then looked at Kearns and said, "You set 'Chico' up." Not only was Kearns shocked, but so were his men.

We later learned the reason for the hit. "Chico" had tried to enter a downtown club owned by a mafia member and was denied. He proceeded to call the owner a motherfucker, which turned out to be the end of the story for "Chico" D'Amico.

9.

A Deadly Arsenal

One of the task force's first assignments regarded a cache of guns and ammo, along with dynamite, buried in the yard of Giambi's Grill, a bar and grill on Bennington Street in East Boston, a place Barboza and company often frequented. We got the call at the DA's office and we immediately bolted to East Boston court. There, we obtained a warrant and proceeded to Giambi's.

I remember thinking nothing of it as we arrived on the scene shortly after noon. Commander Doyle's men, along with the commander of District 7, Captain Francis Quinn, met us there. The bomb squad was digging up the back yard while Domestic Affairs thoroughly searched the premises. I was being pushed around like a pinball in a machine. While bumping into detectives and trying to stay out of the way, I observed a refrigerator and decided to open it to see if there was anything to drink inside. Lo and behold, in the freezer behind the ice cube trays were several loaded clips of M1 ammo.

After I found the ammo in the freezer, the detectives pushed me aside and continued to search the freezer. They found more ammunition for small arms, along with a shotgun and shells, a .38 caliber revolver, a Lugar and a .32 caliber automatic—all loaded. More weapons were stashed behind a loose ceiling panel in a restroom between the bar and kitchen and a club, a baseball bat, a blackjack and a bayonet were found in the cellar. In a box under the counter at the front end of the bar were more small arms slugs including .38 caliber dumdums, some steel-jacketed bullets and several .30 caliber armor-piercing rifle shells.

The detectives talked to the owner of the establishment, Louis D'Amico of East Boston, and he said he knew nothing about the weapons or bullets

Officers examine bullets found in a freezer during the raid of a bar.

found there. He also said that the five-room apartment over the bar had been rented some time ago by Nicholas Femia, but he'd never occupied it—nor had he ever paid any rent. Femia had been locked up in the Charles Street jail (along with Barboza and Patrick Fabiano) for the past several weeks on a gun carrying charge. It was later determined that Femia worked at the bar and grill occasionally as a bartender with his buddy "Chico" D'Amico, who was murdered earlier that week.

All the ammunition and weapons were taken to Boston Police Headquarters and examined by our technicians who determined that the type of gun used to kill "Chico" was a .32 caliber carbine sold by a Florida manufacturer. The detectives and bomb squad found no dynamite at Giambi's, but they did come up with (as they put it) a "small but deadly arsenal of guns and ammunition." The arsenal, detectives were led to believe, was acquired for use in a future gangland murder to avenge the slayings of Arthur "Tash" Bratsos of Medford and Thomas J. DePriscio, Jr. of Roslindale.

All of the men associated with Giambi's were friends of Joe Barboza and were capable of anything, including murder. By recovering the ammunition and weapons we may have prevented a mini-war. Back then no one questioned Commander Doyle's source of information or why he was there in the first place. The newspapers ran a picture of me holding the clips with a caption that read: "Detective finds ammo belonging to gangland figures."

10.

A Threat and Some Luck

STAY AWAY FROM MY HOUSE

One morning as I was about to leave my third-floor apartment to go pick up the boss, my wife asked me to wait a few minutes so she could run to the store. When she got back home, she wore a frightened expression on her face. When I asked her what was wrong, she took me to the window and pointed outside at a white Lincoln parked in front of our house. The driver seemed familiar to her—she had seen his mug shot in my folder. I told her not to worry and headed out to talk to the man in the car.

Going down the stairs, I tried to conceal the shotgun under my trench coat. I made my way to my unmarked car, which was parked in front of the Lincoln. The man behind the wheel called out, "Frankie get in da car!" I instantly recognized him as someone we wanted to talk to concerning the D'Amico murder. We had never talked before, but I did know his face from the many bars and nightclubs we "task forced" (visited). While we had information that this was the guy who had whacked "Chico," we had no evidence. But even though we had nothing on this guy, I knew what he was capable of.

I got in the passenger seat of the car as he stared straight ahead. I held my shotgun partially exposed—just enough for him to see.

He told me I had a beautiful wife and then asked how many kids I had. This thug had been in many bars and nightclubs we "task forced" and although we were both there, we had never talked. I turned and thanked him and gave him a clearer view of my shotgun. He looked at me and asked, "Why are you looking for me?" I told him our boss wanted to talk to him and advised him to go to the DA's office, to which he agreed. As I

Joe "Injun Joe" Conforti and me after an arrest on Somerset St.

got out of the car, I told him he would be making a big mistake if he ever showed up in front of my house again. He seemed to get the message.

TRAFFIC JAM

Meanwhile, in the South Boston-Dorchester area, it was business as usual. Criminals had free reign to conduct illicit activities, from loan-sharking to murder. The task force was becoming increasingly frustrated. We worked day and night trying to pick up members of Barboza's gang for questioning on murders, including that of a local ex-professional boxer, Tony Veranis, whose bullet-riddled body was found in the Blue Hills section of Milton in April 1966.

On March 1, 1967, I, along with task force members McCain and Arria, headed out for a bite to eat. When we were less than a block from the courthouse we could hear police communications coming from a traffic jam in front of us. As luck would have it, we spotted three of the men we were looking for sitting in a car that had been reported stolen. Behind the wheel was Jimmy Kearns who had just been cleared of any complicity in the "Chico" D'Amico killing, though his driver's license had been suspended.

Also in the car were William Kelly of South Boston and Raymond Stillings and Robert Conlin, both of Roxbury. We obtained a search warrant from Chief Justice Elija Adlow and then began to literally tear the car apart. In it we found a ring with 150 master automobile keys, a baseball bat, two tire wrenches, a pinch bar, a set of registration plates, a pocket knife, a switchblade, several wallets, a spent .45 caliber shell and a police transistor radio capable of picking up Boston Police, MDC and State Police frequencies. The men were arrested and charged with possession of burglarious tools, a switchblade and larceny of an automobile. We knew they all worked for the Bennett Brothers and were close to Barboza and Stephen "the Rifleman" Flemmi.

Meanwhile, Barboza, who was sentenced in January 1967 to serve a five-year term on weapons charges in Walpole State Prison, started to talk to Rico and the FBI.

11.

My Return to the TPF

THE LAST STRAW

Once in the middle of the night, my daughter Patty, who was just over three years old, couldn't sleep and she came into our bedroom. As she stood at the foot of our bed trying to wake us, I instinctively grabbed my service revolver (which I kept under the bed) and aimed it at my daughter. What was I doing? Working day and night, not making any money, constantly being threatened and feeling that something just "ain't right" was wearing on me. That was it. The next day, after having some heated words with the boss, I told him I wanted out. I was sick of him telling me who I could or could not talk to and I especially didn't like being called a punk, even though I knew he didn't mean it.

The following month, I knocked on Garrett Byrne's door and asked if I could speak to him. The name Garrett Byrne was renowned throughout the state, especially in Suffolk County. Anyone would be proud to work for him.

"What's the matter, Frankie?" he asked me and I began to mumble like a fool, telling him things and not knowing what he knew. As it turned out there wasn't much he didn't know.

I told him I felt I was a little too young for this job and that maybe I needed more street experience. He said he understood perfectly and that I could come back anytime I wished. He wished me luck and asked if I wanted to go back to my beloved TPF. I said yes and he shook my hand. By this point, I hadn't received my five-year stripe and yet I felt I had already had a full career. Walking out of his office, I felt like someone had taken a huge load off my back.

SUMMER IN BOSTON

The summer months in the downtown area of Boston were filled with many activities. City Hall Plaza was a favorite gathering place. The mayor started a program called "Concerts on the Plaza." The city would put the call out with the help of one of the mayor's best coordinators, a good friend of mine by the name of Patti Pappa, to hire celebrities to entertain on the plaza. Among them were Al Martino, the Everly Brothers and many stars from the past, including one of my personal favorites, the Platters.

Busloads of tourists would arrive at City Hall Plaza to sit back and enjoy the "oldies." After the concert the tourists would gather in the famed and historic Fanueil Hall Marketplace where they could eat and then set off to walk the Freedom Trail by following the guiding red line embedded in the sidewalk. At every historical stop on the trail there was either a historical ranger or a plaque depicting the event that happened there. Some highlights were the site of the Boston Massacre, the Granary Burying Grounds where many of Boston's patriots are buried, the Old State House where the Declaration was read from its balcony and of course Fanueil Hall, where the freedom fighters planned their next move. From there tourists could make their way down to the Paul Revere House and the oldest public square in America, North Square.

At Quincy Market there were always many celebrities walking to a restaurant after a performance at one of Boston's many theaters. Middleweight Champion of the World, "Marvelous" Marvin Hagler, noted Quincy Market as one of his favorite places to go. He enjoyed talking and being recognized and the tourists loved him. Eventually Hagler and I became good friends.

Around the corner from Paul Revere's house is the main street of the North End, Little Italy, where there are 128 restaurants and not a single bad one. During the summer there were festivals in the street on every weekend. Different Catholic Saints were honored: the patron saint of provinces in Italy whose residents moved into Little Italy. The North End has the lowest crime rate per capita than any other part of our commonwealth. While walking the streets, with their cobblestone alleys and squares, it was easy to imagine the colonist sauntering into the Old North Church with its majestic tower, or looking up at the "one if by land, two if by sea" lantern in the Christ Church steeple to see whether the British were coming by land or sea and then to visualize that infamous midnight ride of Paul Revere to warn the country folk of impending danger.

Paul Revere's House.

Reunited

On July 7, 1967, I returned to the TPF under Captain Bradley's command. After a brief welcome, it was back to the patrol car and back with Gerry. While we made small talk and tried to get used to each other again, Gerry told me things had been going smoothly for him and nothing really exciting had happened.

"Not even a dead body," he said, smiling.

Gerry was a smart street kid from the Bronx, so when I started telling him about the goings-on in the DA's office, he got it. Gerry never wanted to be a detective. He knew that the temptation was there and if he saw something he didn't like, he'd probably lose his temper.

The TPF was responsible for guarding dignitaries. On July 30, Vice President Humphrey was escorted by the TPF to the Sheraton Boston Hotel for a Democratic dinner. He was the first of the many celebrities I would eventually escort.

Shirley MacLaine

That winter, Shirley MacLaine came to Boston for her debut in *Sweet Charity*. Her agent called headquarters and asked for two TPF men to assist her during her stay at the Sheraton Plaza Hotel. It was a cold, snowy week and the agent requested to have one man inside and one man outside. Officer

"Red" Skelton (center) filming at the waterfront; George Simms, Gene Simpson, me and Gerry Meehan.

Al Martino entertaining at City Hall Plaza, with me.

Me and Jackie Mason at Quincy Market.

Al Osso, the eldest, asked me if he could be inside because he was a fan of Shirley's.

What happened next was bizarre. Miss MacLaine exited the hotel through the side door to do some shopping. As she was attempting to cross the street she had to climb a snowbank and she got stuck. I immediately ran to her aid. She held out her arms as I climbed the snowbank and helped her down. As this was happening, an alert photographer took a picture of us descending the snowbank. Appearing on the front page of the old *Record American* the next day was a photo of us holding hands with the caption, "Gallant Boston Police Officer Frank DeSario aids Shirley MacLaine out of snowbank." The next night I escorted her to the theater for her grand opening. She wrote down my name, gave me a hug and said goodbye after the show.

A few years later, I was in my kitchen watching the *Good Morning Show* when the host, Joyce Kilhawick, introduced her guest Shirley MacLaine. I poked my wife and told her that I knew Shirley. Joyce asked Shirley, "Have you ever been in Boston before?"

Ms. MacLaine replied, "The last time I was in Boston I was greeted by a handsome Boston policeman and I believe his name was Frank."

With that they took a commercial break and our phone rang. It was Joyce Kilhawick and she told me that Shirley MacLaine wanted to speak

(Herald Traveler Staff Photo by Frank Kelly)

GALLANT Boston Police officer Frank DeSario helps screen actress Shirley MacLaine over snowbank yesterday in front of Sheraton Plaza Hotel. She was here for world premiere of her latest film, "Sweet Charity."

Helping Shirley MacLaine over a snowbank.

Geri and me backstage with Shirley MacLaine.

with me. Shirley got on the phone and asked me how I'd been. Meanwhile, as I was breaking into a cold sweat looking at my family, she started telling the audience how wonderful and charming I was and how I had saved her from the snowbank. She said there would be two tickets at the box office in the Wang Center for me and a guest, then blew me a kiss and said, "See you later."

The next night, my wife and I were escorted to the front row in the Wang Center for the opening of *That's Entertainment*.

Shirley came onstage wearing a female version of a tuxedo and began her song and dance routine. At the end of her first number, she paused for a sip of water while her audience gave her a standing ovation. She told the audience how much she loved Boston and then shared the story of how a Boston police officer had pulled her out of a snowbank on her last visit. She then introduced me and invited me onto the stage, where she serenaded me. I turned three shades of red and there was a loud applause. She invited my wife and me backstage after the show.

After meeting and talking with her backstage we thanked her for an outstanding night and told her how much we enjoyed her show. At the end of our visit, my wife asked Shirley, "Did you have anything to do with my husband?"

I was thinking she would obviously say no, but Shirley smiled and said, "I'll never tell." Then she winked at my wife.

How could this duty possibly compare to being on the murderous streets of Dorchester and Roxbury—at the same pay?

12.

The Lingering DA's Office

Try to be Brave

The streets of Boston are different at night. It always seemed that the darker it got, the more unfriendly the citizens would be—that the good people would go indoors before dark. This is when the Tactical Patrol Force would start its shift.

The TPF was freed of routine patrol so that it could aggressively go after the most serious crimes. This was our world. The best part of being in this unit was that we had the freedom to go from one district to another depending on where the action was. The high visibility created by the TPF, I'm sure, deterred crimes that otherwise might have happened.

The TPF was unique. It was trained to perform any function that the department had in mind. We could be called to fill-in at any district that was short in manpower. Vice and Narcotics would borrow some of our men to act as decoys and work undercover for drug buys. We worked the whole city, whereas the districts had to maintain their manpower numbers to keep their areas safe. There was always a bit of jealousy between the TPF men and the District men, maybe because they knew we were handpicked and were part of the Mounted Patrol, Harbor Patrol and later the Motorcycle Unit. It was truly a young man's job and, man, were these guys dedicated!

The TPF gave me the opportunity to visit the haunts of the crime bosses I had investigated while in the DA's office. The bad guys, it seemed, had no fear of an approaching squad car, even as it pulled in front of their establishments. But let an unmarked car come close and they would disappear.

A hostage situation—three people and the gunman were killed.

In a way I was lucky I had learned so much (probably too much). In the short time I spent in the DA's office I learned more than what a patrol officer might learn in a career, simply because I had the resources and associated with the upper echelon.

Working day and night in the DA's office and saturating the Roxbury-Dudley Street area as well as South Boston, I was well aware of the likes of Stevie "the Rifleman" Flemmi and his cohorts, as well as Bulger's crew in South Boston and the goings-on in the North End.

END OF THE BARBOZA CHASE

When I left the task force I thought I was finally through with gangland activity, but I still found myself involved in so many things related to the DA's office. When Barboza was spilling his guts, lying and sending innocent men to jail at Suffolk Superior Court, my SWAT team and I were outside the courtroom protecting him. At the time, the names he was giving up meant nothing to me, so I assumed that they were indeed murderers or co-conspirators. But I did find it ironic that after chasing "the Animal" for so long, there I was protecting him. I couldn't help but think about all the times we almost had him.

During Barboza's testimony, everything seemed to be elementary. Throughout his testimony, he was able to get even with a lot of his ex-associates in the North End, especially the Angiullos, calmly aware that there was a $50,000 tag on his head and that he was going to avenge "Chico's" murder (for which he knew Angiullo and his associates were responsible). Barboza sent innocent men to prison for life, while secretly he was in alliance with Bulger, Flemmi, Rico and FBI agent John Connolly. And he knew that he was going to be relocated to another state under an assumed name. Local law didn't care much as they assumed Barboza was telling the truth and regardless, the city of Boston would finally be rid of "the Animal."

When Barboza was finishing up his testimony at Suffolk Superior Court, we had at least one squad of police officers on every floor of the courthouse and the outside was surrounded by SWAT teams. We had to call for some outside help, just in case. We knew Barboza had enemies right down the street, less than a mile away in the North End and his friends in Revere and East Boston were either in the can or hiding, but only he knew the true severity of the situation. At the time, we didn't know for sure the nature of his affiliation with Flemmi and Bulger. Barboza was escorted out of the courthouse, down the stairs and into the "tombs" where a few years earlier he had been booked and locked up for at least half a day. Now we were finally getting rid of Joe Barboza. It wasn't exactly the way we'd hoped to end our relationship but at least we were getting him out of Boston.

The Boston papers were covering the event like it was the World Series. Rumors around Boston Police Headquarters were that a top lieutenant in the local mafia by the name of Joseph Russo had a contract on "the Animal." Now he belonged to the Feds. It was their responsibility to relocate him and place him in a witness protection program where he would live under an assumed name.

Barboza was known to have killed at least forty people and he enjoyed the notoriety. He was so bad that he once killed a man who had witnessed him murdering a guy by the name of Romeo Martin. The poor witness worked for a soft drink company and he was loading a machine when he saw Barboza in action. When Barboza noticed the witness, he walked over to him and shot him dead, in spite of the man's pleas for his life. While questioning a friend of Barboza's, we heard that "the Animal" once said that when he clipped someone "it was like fucking Marilyn Monroe."

In 1969 Barboza was told to leave Massachusetts forever, and "the Animal," we later found out, headed to the West Coast and continued in his murderous ways—at least two more times in the San Francisco area. It appeared that he must have felt invincible and he began to let down his guard. He finally got what he deserved. One beautiful day in February 1976, as he was getting out of a vehicle, a shotgun blast ended his life. This was the end of Joseph "the Animal" Barboza. Word got out quickly in Boston and the celebrations began. I remember how we celebrated that night. He was no loss to the community.

13.

TPF Tales

Too Close to Home

I remember one night—it was the Wednesday of the first week of October 1968. I was out patrolling Roxbury and looking at the house where I grew up. I was in a daze thinking about all the good times I had and the people I knew as a youth when I received a call from my brother Mike, who with a glazed voice told me that our dad, a Roxbury oil dealer, had been lured into an apartment after delivering fuel oil at the corner of Blue Hill Avenue and Alaska Street and he was slugged, stomped and robbed at gunpoint of $585.

After Mike assured me that my father would be all right, I raced down to District 9 on Dudley Street to talk to the investigating officers. A short time later my brother arrived and we both read the police report. It seemed this maggot pulled a gun on my dad and lured him into an apartment on Blue Hill Avenue. He ordered my dad to beg for his life while putting a gun in his mouth. He then pistol-whipped him, took his money and fled.

Mike became so enraged that it took two of us to keep him from storming out of the station and taking vengeance on his own. Luckily we calmed him down and convinced him to ride with us to visit the scene.

My fellow officers learned of the incident and offered their free time to help investigate. My friends had plenty of leads, but an arrest was never made. This was lucky for the assailant because he was spared a meeting with my brother Mike.

Word spread through the community that a TPF officer's father was stomped, beaten and robbed and many people voiced their concern. Dad, in his day, would have showed that maggot where to put that gun, but he wasn't a young man anymore.

My father recovered, but I'm sure that incident forced him to retire. One thing was clear: Roxbury, my hometown, a place where no one locked their doors when I was a kid, had changed.

MY FIRST SHOT

As a young officer I always wondered if I would ever have to use my service revolver and hoped that if I did, I would be justified. On March 21, 1969, at 12:30 a.m., I stopped wondering.

That night, Gerry and I were on a walking beat in the Combat Zone area where just about anything could happen. This was an area loaded with pimps, junkies and motorcycle gangs.

Walking in the vicinity of Beach and Washington Streets, a white male came running toward Gerry and me, yelling "Help! Help! He's got a gun!" Gerry and I cautiously ran up LaGrange Street where, sure enough, in the middle of the street, a man stood holding a gun and aiming it in our direction.

"Don't come any closer or I will kill you!" he yelled. He repeated that statement two more times while running toward us and firing his gun. I ran for cover behind a parked car. I was so nervous I dropped my gun. I didn't want to take my eyes off him. As he stood no more than fifteen or twenty feet from me, I yelled for him to drop his gun and he fired in our direction.

Fast as lightning, Gerry pushed two unknown white males out of the line of fire and yelled at the assailant to drop his gun. Again the suspect yelled, "Don't come any closer!" He continued to walk slowly in my direction with his gun pointed at me.

I knew as he was getting close that I was going to have to shoot. Slowly taking aim and putting my revolver in single action mode, I kept thinking, "Am I right?" Then my gun seemed to explode. Looking up, I saw the gunman still standing with his gun still in his hand. I thought, "Could I be such a lousy shot?" Then he dropped to the ground, even now gripping his gun. I watched as Officer Dominic Fontana ran to the suspect and took the gun out of his hand. It was a loaded eight-shot automatic. I remember hearing sirens blaring from all directions and I kept hoping that I had done the right thing.

Sergeant Detective Feeney approached me out of the darkness and proceeded to console me. He told me that he had observed the scene and that I was justified in shooting back. The assailant survived the shooting and it was time to get back to work.

After the shooting incident on LaGrange St.

Me and Geri at my retirement party at City Hall Plaza.

"Community relations" with neighborhood kids.

Mary Brown

Later that summer, Gerry and I got a call to investigate a possible suicide at the Massachusetts Transit Authority rapid transit station at Dover and Washington Streets. Off we went, two big tough TPF men responding to a simple call. The lifeless body of a woman lay on the third rail. After the proper authorities had left, it was our job to remove the body. The problem was that she was stuck—and she was 350 pounds. Not an easy task, but we finally managed to get her into the police wagon. We headed to the Boston City Hospital where she was officially pronounced dead on arrival. Now it was time to go to the morgue.

I had never been to the morgue before so I didn't know what to expect. Gerry was so white I thought he was going to faint. I backed into the receiving ramp to deliver the body. Opening the wagon door, I jumped in to make sure the sheet we put over the body was secure. Gerry was outside holding the "litter," which was positioned headfirst toward him. I was in the back moving toward Gerry when somehow I managed to step on the sheet, keeping it from going forward with the body. Gerry came nose-to-nose with the uncovered body, practically kissing it, while we put it on a gurney, rolled it to the receiving door and rang the bell. To our surprise, there stood an intern dressed in white, wearing tong shoes and eating a tuna sandwich.

The next thing I remember was seeing Gerry keeled over outside, throwing up his guts. Upon seeing this, I proceeded to do the same. We then headed back to the station to fill out the report for the family and make a copy for us.

Going home that night, I felt worse than I'd felt in years. I couldn't sleep so I got up early in the morning to have coffee with my wife. Sitting at the breakfast table, she said, "By the way, you got a phone call this morning." I asked who it was, and she told me it was Mary Brown, which was the name of the woman we had taken off the third rail.

"What the hell are you talking about?" I asked her. Geri said that Mary Brown had called to tell me that it was all a big mistake.

My wife had found my report on my desk and decided to have some fun with it.

Park Square Beat

Things were going great. It was almost the end of 1969. I had a steady walking beat on Park Square. The year before, Park Square had been a haven for hookers, pimps, truck stops and cop fighters. It belonged to District 4 and they needed help to clean it up. Now it belonged to the TPF.

In the square were Hayes Bickford Cafeteria, a Waldorf and a Child's Restaurant. These were places where every creep in the area would hang out. I volunteered to walk the beat but my partner, Gerry, wanted to stay in a cruiser. The TPF walked two abreast, so now I had to find a new partner.

Paul Moscone was a kid from East Boston who had been a clerk until now but wanted some fresh air. Paul and I made some good grabs in the square. We made arrests for handbag snatches, fights, assault and battery and prostitution. It was real dirty work. It was no surprise that District 4 didn't want it.

Miraculously, it seemed that overnight the Waldorf closed, as did Hayes Bickford Cafeteria and the truck stop. Taking their place was a new Bunny Club, Bachelors III and the Great Gatsby. Now with the Statler Hilton Hotel in the middle, Park Square had become a glamorous walking beat. Needless to say, there was a line of cops outside the captain's office wanting to walk Park Square. What a great place to work, especially Bachelors III, a spot all the sports figures frequented. The principal owners were Jimmy Colclough, the former great receiver for the Boston Patriots, and the one and only Joe Namath. Athletes from every sport would eventually make an appearance there, including Derek Sanderson who may have had a small piece of the action. Derek played number sixteen center iceman for Boston Bruin Hockey and made "Rookie of the Year." He was born in Ontario, Canada, but became one of the most admired athletes in the U.S. and was popular with all of Boston. Everyone loved Derek.

I met Derek while I was walking the beat in Park Square. He was unfamiliar at first with the area and he would often ask me what places to avoid. After his career with the Bruins ended, Derek worked for the Boston Police Athletic League (PAL). Derek could almost fly on the ice. In fact, I would often say that when Derek walked he moved like he was on ice. Derek and I became the best of friends. He had such a great personality and would talk to anyone. Every time I asked him for an autograph for some kid he'd always oblige and he never failed to show up when the Patrolman's Association was doing something special for the kids.

14.

The Brighton Police

Big Changes

The Deer Island House of Correction inmates started acting up. Their personnel took care of the situation but they still needed TPF assistance. On the way down, our new commander, Captain Moe Allen, asked the troops not to wear their side arms into the prison. Well there was some controversy over whether this was the right thing to do. Ignoring the captain's suggestion not to carry a weapon led to my transfer.

I had gone from the TPF to the District Attorney's Office, Homicide, to what we called the "Brighton Police." This district was considered to be a country club compared to where I was previously assigned. Brighton had a population of about eighty-five thousand people comprised mostly of college students. It was bordered by Boston College and Boston University, so the biggest problems in the area came from student drinking. The students who didn't live on campus had apartments in the hundreds of brick four-story buildings within a mile of their schools. Therefore, parking was also a major problem. It was not unusual to see the Boston Fire Department's district chief patrolling the area along with our patrol cars. It was a major priority that these streets remain open in case of fire, so dealing with the illegal parking was a consistent problem.

There I was after ten years with the department—they had decided to deprogram me, giving me a break. Computers were now running all departments and all reports were now done electronically. New rules and regulations were in effect and the training of the new recruits was more sophisticated. With all of these changes, both the old and the new were having trouble adjusting. I was labeled "old school" and I knew it would soon be time to go.

But this was not to be.

MISTAKEN IDENTITY

I had a new partner, Mikey Flemmi; a cop with a great record who had been through all the riots. He had made some great arrests and was popular with all the guys. He was also from Roxbury and had grown up about two miles from me.

It was 1973 and Mike and I were partners in a sector car. Mike was a great wheelman and he never let me drive. I remember chasing stolen cars down the narrow streets of Brighton, in the Allston area, never getting into an accident and always getting our man. Mikey was, and still is, one of my best friends. He was always a good man to back you up. But Mike had a stigma attached to him from his first day on the job.

Mikey was the kid brother of two of Boston's most ferocious killers. His oldest brother, Vincent J. "Jimmy the Bear" Flemmi, was an enforcer for the Bennett Brothers in Roxbury. He was a loud, intimidating sort whose mere presence made you shudder. The law finally caught up with him and he was sent to Walpole State Prison where one of his rivals stabbed him to death.

Mikey's other brother, Stephen "the Rifleman" Flemmi, had been a hero in the Korean War. As a paratrooper, he jumped behind enemy lines in Korea and as a sniper he eliminated many of the enemy brass. Stevie was a handsome, quiet guy who always wore a smile and who could "make" any girl. He was so ruthless, his reputation was: don't get him angry with you or it will be goodbye. Stevie was so good at his trade that the big bad guys loved him. What made him so dangerous was that he could turn on you in an instant, as was the case with the Bennett Brothers. They gave Stevie his first break and then he eliminated all three of them.

Mikey Flemmi didn't have a chance. He wanted no part of what his brothers were doing but they were his family. Mike knew that I had been part of the DA task force, yet he never once asked me how things were going up there. And never once do I recall having a single conversation about his brothers, even though he knew that I knew they were as bad as one could imagine.

The night the third Bennett brother got killed his body had been thrown into a snowbank on Harvard Street near Blue Hill Avenue in the Dorchester area. When the local sector car received the call and officers turned the body over without recognizing him, they observed what appeared to be a .38 caliber pistol, similar to what our detectives carry. I was working a cruiser that night and because the guys in the sector knew I was familiar with the gangland killings, they called me to see if I knew the victim. Their main concern was to make sure the victim was not a police detective. With the aid of Officers John Lyndstone and Marty Coleman, I identified the victim as William Bennett, the third of the Bennett brothers.

For years no one knew who killed the Bennetts. I remember the families begging for help from the locals to find out who had killed their loved ones. The law had always suspected Stevie, but how could he do that? Stevie supposedly loved the Bennetts.

One night Mike and I were in the 14-1 on patrol with Mike driving, of course, when we receive a radio dispatch for shots fired in the vicinity of Saint Columbkille's Church. We pulled up to the scene within a few minutes and, after a quick search of the area, found nothing and cleared the call.

A short time later, the dispatcher called and said that the nuns in the convent were concerned and could we return and investigate further. We went back to the area and there on the sidewalk on Sparhawk Street, opposite Saint Columbkille's Church, was a car riddled with bullets, apparently from a machine gun. The driver had been bleeding profusely and was obviously dead. He was a local bartender by the name of Michael Milano. Also in the car were a seriously wounded white male, identified as Louis LaPiana and, screaming in the back seat, an unidentified white female who had been shot but whose wound did not appear life-threatening.

I can remember writing out the report with Mikey, never thinking this had anything to do with the Winter Hill Gang or anyone else that I knew. None of the victims had police records so it was assumed that it was a case of mistaken identity. For years the case went unsolved, although many had their suspicions. That is, until Whitey Bulger's right-hand man, Kevin Weeks, started "ratting out" everyone. After certain hit men learned that Bulger and company were informants for the FBI, Agent Rico and others, Johnny Martarano turned against them and admitted to the mistaken identity hit on Michael Milano and friends. LaPiana was paralyzed for the rest of his life and died in 2001.

15

Motorcycle Patrol

BUSING AND INTEGRATION

As 1973 was coming to an end, I decided to slow down a bit. I was lucky enough to get transferred to night motorcycle duty—a great job. The hardest thing I had to do was get the Saturday night paper for the boss. That job didn't last long.

In 1974 Judge Arthur Garrity ordered that Boston schools be desegregated by busing thousands of black children into white neighborhoods. This move incited a great deal of racial turmoil, particularly in South Boston. In response, Judge Garrity mobilized all the motorcycle police into one unit, forming Mobile Operation Patrol (MOP). Our main function was to ensure the safety and welfare of children involved with school busing. This was somewhat of a historical event and the rest of the country watched to see if the busing would be a success. It wasn't.

The only ones who benefited were the bus companies. The kids were scared to death and learned nothing. Parents mobilized local politicians and agitated crowds who took out their frustrations on the police. This was not only in South Boston but in the black school districts as well. There they were, South Boston natives, yelling and cursing at the TPF and MOP as if we were responsible for forced busing. Some crowd members were even parents of police officers on the TPF and MOP.

The elders got the younger people riled up to the extent that it became vicious. The high school was located on a hill known as Dorchester Heights, and as winter moved in and the temperature dropped, some of the radicals opened hydrants early in the morning, flooding and later icing the streets to prevent us from ascending the hills leading to South Boston High.

Because of these tactics some of our bikes went down and some officers ended up in the hospital. Many of us were pelted with rocks. This lasted for over three years. Some of our officers had heart attacks and died, while others sustained serious injuries from bike accidents as a result of these attacks.

The TPF and MOP spent every school day working throughout the city protecting our kids, while at night we patrolled the troubled areas. We were averaging over 200 hours a month. In one month, I accumulated 250 hours of overtime. During daytime bus escorts, bikers would return to the staging area, put their rain gear on the radio receiver and their boots on the saddlebags (without taking them off) and take a quick nap. At night, we patrolled Southie and Charlestown, breaking up fights and gangs of thugs throwing bricks at police vehicles, MTA buses and even at a car they thought carried blacks.

After surviving the LaGrange Street shooting and the years chasing Barboza and company, I thought there was no way I was going to get hurt chasing kids. Boy was I wrong.

When we patrolled the streets, we worked in squads of five men with a squad leader. One night I approached an intersection leading into Bunker Hill Street when all of a sudden I was knocked from my motorcycle and started bleeding from my forehead and eye. The protestors had hung piano wire with the intent to take down our bikes.

Riding behind me was Cycle Officer Frank Megnia who watched me go down and came to my rescue. He held my head while flagging down an ambulance that had been assigned to that area. The force of hitting the wire caused my helmet visor to split, breaking the impact. The wire still caused some bleeding to my head and my eyelid was slightly torn. Thank God we had ambulances standing by.

The next day, our captain, John Dow, told me the FBI had been notified and was on its way down to interview me. They assured me that they would get whoever was responsible, but I never heard from them again.

Back on the street, I was called into South Boston High to break up a fight between blacks and whites. Some of the classrooms were in session and it was amazing to see students with their feet up on the desks with the teacher standing by and doing nothing about it. I believe that in over three years of busing these kids learned absolutely nothing. I remember their troubled faces as they waved at me while I escorted them to and from school.

In October 1974 there was an incident at the Rabbit Inn, a drinking hole for the locals. Daily, buses carrying blacks away from school were pelted with rocks as they passed the Rabbit Inn. When the TPF found out what was happening, we took action. Unfortunately, the locals complained to the

On patrol at Quincy Market. The historic Custom House is in the background.

Boston Police Drill Team.

politicians and they in turn wanted action against the police. In a small way they won and busing finally ended.

In 1978 community leaders in the Roxbury-Dorchester area determined that the TPF was too aggressive in its tactics. With pressure mounting on City Hall the TPF was disbanded. A new unit was formed under the command of Lieutenant Bob Hayden. He picked his own men and went into troubled areas where gang members harassed transit bus drivers. Members of Hayden's squad began boarding these buses and stacked the sidewalks with weapons—guns, switchblades, ammo and in many instances automatic handguns.

As time went by, the squad became more and more aggressive. Eventually, the very same leaders who wanted relief from crime in their neighborhoods went screaming to City Hall that Hayden's men were too aggressive and Hayden's squad was disbanded. As the months went by, crime was back on the rise and the leaders again yelled for more police presence.

But with Hayden and the TPF gone, whom could they call if an emergency arose?

ENTER SPECIAL OPERATIONS

I was disappointed to see my beloved TPF and MOP dissolved, but what I didn't know was that the planning and research department, along with the brass, was forming a Special Operations Patrol. This unit was to consist of former members of the TPF and MOP. It had everything—motorcycles, mounted patrol and a bomb squad—all under the direction of Superintendent Robert Bradley and Deputy Superintendent Martin Mulkern.

The motorcycle division's primary patrol function varied. The bikes worked in pairs, saturating the city while issuing traffic citations and backing up the district cars. In a way, it reminded me of the old TPF. Here we were, again in training, working with three-foot batons. But now we had brand new Harley Davidson motorcycles, new Glock semi-automatics with ultra-penetrating ammunition and were trained as teams for use in SWAT situations. The purpose of the teams was to ensure that we always had at least one SWAT team working at night.

This new organization was a far cry from the TPF SWAT team that some thought was the first in the country. I can recall hundreds of times being activated for an entry, putting on our SWAT get-up and loading into the wagon with the team without knowing where we were going. Then we'd arrive and were hurriedly apprised of the situation and how to gain entry.

Pope John Paul at the Boston Common.

Many times we got what we were looking for without incident. Other times we were met by suspects who refused to drop their weapons. Luckily, my team always prevailed.

One time, while trying to gain entry to one of the apartments in the Franklin Park project, I was supposed to be the second man in with my shotgun. I tripped. Down to the ground I went while five other SWAT members trampled over me. After that I was the talk of the unit.

Later that summer, Special Operations received word that the Pope was coming to Boston. I remember the thrill of being a part of the team that met the Pope at Logan Airport and being on his left side as he descended from his Alitalia jumbo jet. He gave us all his blessing. On our motorcycles, we escorted him through the Sumner Tunnel and then to Saint John's Seminary in Brighton. After a short visit he came out and we escorted him to the Cathedral of the Holy Cross.

As we escorted him back from the cathedral, I pulled up from behind and came face to face with him. The Pope acknowledged me and handed me a white rose. I gently kissed the rose and laid it ever so gently into my right saddlebag. Then it was off to the Boston Common and an outside mass attended by thousands.

16.

Corruption

Looking back and reminiscing about the old days, I can't help but realize how naive I really was. Sure, I was street smart, a pretty tough kid who always thought he could handle any situation. If I couldn't, I knew my brothers would be there to back me up. With the TPF, I knew that if I was ever in trouble and in need of assistance, all I had to do was get to my radio to put in an "officer in trouble" call. I never had to worry about my back being covered while working with the SWAT team either. Relying on officers you could trust helped with the success of all those entries we made. But a few months after my retirement the newspapers began breaking stories of corruption. There was FBI corruption, a few dirty state cops, maybe one Boston cop who ended up in jail and a detective whom we thought was beyond reproach.

There I was on a bright, sunny summer day reading about all this dirt that had been going on while I had been in the DA's office. After thirty-five years on the job, I finally learned the truth: other law enforcement personnel were on the side of the murderers, and FBI agent John Connolly played a significant part in this. It made me sick to think about the actions of such a dirty FBI agent as Connolly. I could understand how Bulger groomed Connolly and made him what he was for his own particular purpose. But understanding Connolly's motives was beyond my grasp. Although Connolly was making big bucks (so much that he wasn't even cashing his paychecks) and living a luxurious life, no one had ever heard of him.

It seems that all hell broke loose when the squeeze was put on some of Whitey Bulger's bagmen. Fearing that they would have to do time, they started making deals. They told of the whereabouts of bodies buried in the greater Boston area, and with the help of Bulger's number one man, Kevin

Former FBI agent, John Connolly.

Retirement party at City Hall Plaza; me, Commissioner Paul Evans and Mayor Tom Mennino.

Weeks, they described how people were killed by Bulger and Flemmi while under the protection of Connolly. Sadly, anyone who dared go to the FBI with information that could nail Bulger ended up dead.

But Bulger wasn't the only one being protected. Connolly, with the help of Flemmi, was walking the streets of the North End. The farthest thing from anyone's mind was the possibility that Flemmi was a rat. Well, it turned out he was, big-time, and he helped take down the local mafia boss and his brothers. To think of all those nights we were riding and searching and coming up with nothing. We would receive phone calls in the daytime regarding the whereabouts of friends of Barboza that inevitably turned out to be fruitless.

To this day, that knowledge makes my blood boil. In a way I started feeling angry with myself for not being suspicious enough to ask more questions. Did Lieutenant Ingenere know something and not tell us? Why weren't we allowed to talk to Domestic Affairs? How did Commander Doyle always beat us to a murder scene? Could H. Paul Rico have had a contact in the DA's office? But now I know that I did the best I could. My thoughts would shift to all of those men who were wrongly accused and convicted of murder and the pain their families endured. What men like Rico and Connolly did was not just protect vicious killers; they ruined innocent men and their families.

But I keep hoping that maybe something good might come out of all this. I'm sure every law enforcement agency, including the coveted FBI, could learn from past mistakes.

17.

Reflection

Good Times

It is easy to think about the good times I had on the job. It's hard to express just how fraternal this job really is. It is so "tight" that it gets to the point where you don't want to associate with anyone other than cops. And our wives have to be of a certain breed. Without a doubt, the hardest job in the world is being married to a cop. The parties we had, especially while on the TPF, were always so much fun that even the wives enjoyed themselves. We were like a family. When the TPF is lucky enough have a reunion it's always a bunch of guys hugging and reminiscing about how good we were while the wives have the time of their lives.

One officer I will never forget is TPF Officer Bob Guiney, my closest brother on the job, who ironically inherited my badge number (#1) for taking over as senior officer in the department. I can remember one night in the Combat Zone I was getting off duty and walking to my car when I was jumped and kicked to the ground by a group I had investigated for possession of drugs. Upon arrival of the police, the assailants ran off in different directions and made a getaway. Guiney was familiar with the Combat Zone and had a great pipeline—he knew almost every thug in the area—and he aided me in identifying my assailants. That I will never forget.

I remember walking the aisle of the Greyhound bus terminal while performing an extra paid detail when all of a sudden I received a tap on the back. I turned and was knocked to the ground by an ex-boxer who later stated he just wanted to punch a cop. Someone put in a call of "officer in trouble" and while I was on the floor two TPF officers, Ronnie Monroe

Me and Bob Guiney at Downtown Crossing.

and John Patuto, arrived and observed the assailant continuing to throw punches. Well, Ronnie was one tough six-footer and "Big" John was six-four and 250 pounds. As my fellow officers approached, my assailant took one look at them and he immediately surrendered. Just the look of the two officers made him think twice about what he wanted to do.

And I'll never forget my partner for the last five years of my career, Roger "The Dodger" DeMinico, my motorcycle partner in the downtown crossing and Nick Saggesse, another TPF officer who you didn't want to break the law in front of. These are only a few of the men who made the TPF what it was. I never had to worry knowing these guys had my back. So when I say we were like family that was what it was all about.

AND BAD TIMES

But there are also the bad times. In my thirty-nine and a half years on the job I lost many friends who either got seriously hurt or were killed in the line of duty. Since I joined the department, seventeen of my brother officers were killed or died from injuries sustained in the line of duty.

So many dangerous situations arose that we were called on to subdue. We knew we were good and ready for any situation. In the early days of the TPF when we were called in to assist officers in other parts of the city there was always a sense of unwelcome when we entered their precinct area. We were there mostly because they were shorthanded and at times overrun with serious calls. Though in the beginning they sort of resented us, word got out about how quickly we responded, especially when a deafening radio call of "officer in trouble" came in. Word spread so fast that more district commanders started requesting our assistance. I remember patrolling the "hotspots," (areas where there was serious gang activity), in our cruisers with "TPF" initialed on both side fenders and hearing the whisper of "Watch it, it's the TPF."

As time went by, some of our guys were studying for promotion and some wanted to move to slower or less active precincts. New younger cops were volunteering for the TPF. Jerry Hurley, a well-liked, unassuming guy who always wore a wide Irish grin on his handsome face was given the opportunity to transfer to the bomb squad, a dangerous but not as active job as the TPF. He had several years under his belt on the TPF, so after talking it over with his beautiful wife Cynthia, he decided to transfer.

I remember approaching Area A, District 1—Jerry was coming out as I was going in— and I said to him, "Jerry, you're leaving the TPF?"

"It's time to slow down a bit for the sake of my wife and small kids," he told me.

FIGHT FOR LIFE: Police and emergency personnel speed fatally wounded Patrolman Thomas Rose (inset) into Massachusetts General Hospital for emergency surgery last night. AP photo

Assisting Tommy Rose outside Massachusetts General Hospital.

I agreed with him, wished him luck and off we both went. Unfortunately, he was killed by a bomb blast in Roslindale in October 1991 as he was investigating "suspicious persons." Later, I remembered that conversation we had. For some reason Jerry was not someone you expected to get killed. He was so smart and street savvy. He was so well liked. The police community lost a good one.

Officer Roy Sergei was killed chasing a felony suspect through an alley in the South End after responding to a call of "breaking and entering" on October 7, 1987.

Officer Tommy Gil, a marine who served in Vietnam, was struck and killed by an Amtrak train on February 10, 1988 as he searched for guns taken during a Brighton housebreak. Tommy was a South Boston native, handsome, always smiling, with lots of friends. I remember thinking that guys like Tommy would live forever.

Officer Sherman Griffiths was shot in the head during a drug bust on February 17, 1988.

GRIM DUTY: Boston Police Commissioner Francis 'Mickey' Roache talks with reporters outside Massachusetts General Hospital last night following the death of Officer Thomas Rose. Boston Mayor Raymond L. Flynn listens in background. Staff photo by Justine Ellement

Commissioner Francis "Mickey" Roache addresses reporters outside Massachusetts General Hospital following the death of Thomas Rose; Mayor Raymond L. Flynn listens in behind him.

Bucky Johnson was a traffic cop doing his thing at the corner of Tremont and Stuart Streets. He was always smiling and joking with the motorists as they passed by him. One day, he was approached by a citizen who reported a fight in the Tam Cafe, a joint across from Bucky's traffic post. But the citizen failed to tell Bucky that a gun was involved, and Officer Johnson was shot dead. I was a young officer then and I remember what a strong impact that shooting had on me.

One incident that is embedded in my mind occurred on February 19, 1993. It was a Friday night just before roll call. In the guardroom as I was getting ready for first half duty at Area A-1, I was joking and telling stories before hopping on the elevator for the ride down to the garage to begin my motorcycle patrol downtown. While I was getting on the elevator, Officer Tommy Rose was getting off.

"See ya later, Frankie," he said to me.

"Marvelous" Marvin Hagler, ex-middleweight champ, and me.

In the garage, I was putting my gear into the saddlebags on my bike when I heard two loud bangs. I thought nothing of it at first, but then all hell broke loose. Tommy was shot by a prisoner upstairs near the booking area while escorting him to make his one phone call. Tommy was rushed to an ambulance and instead of going on patrol I escorted him to the Massachusetts General Hospital emergency room. I stayed with him as they wheeled him into the operating room. The doctors were optimistic at first, but Tommy died on the operating table.

I recall so vividly escorting the funeral of Walter Schroeder, who was shot in the back and killed while responding to a bank alarm in Brighton on Western Avenue. During the funeral, the killer, William "Lefty" Kilday, was spotted by the State Police on the Massachusetts Turnpike and was pursued with sirens blaring. We were on Market Street escorting Walter and listening on our walkie-talkies as they nabbed the guy. Walter's brother John, a detective in the South End, was killed while investigating holdups in that area.

Fortunately, the good times outweighed the bad times. I had the honor of escorting President Lyndon Johnson, Vice President Hubert Humphrey

Me and two other officers, with Baseball Hall of Famer Carl Yastrzemski.

and the Pope, as well as countless high-profile politicians, movie stars and sports celebrities. In the visitor's dugout while on duty at Fenway Park, I met the manager of the Texas Rangers during their first year in the American League. It was Ted Williams, my idol. Those are fond memories.

18.

North End and "the Goodfellas"

LOCAL COLOR

My last ten years on the job patrolling the North End turned out to be the best years of my career. I had an edge in gaining the confidence of the residents and businessmen there, being one hundred percent Italian and making it clear that I demanded respect. I found that these people spoke their minds, told it like it was, and loved the better things in life. Like most neighborhoods, the theme in the North End was "do right by us and we'll do right by you."

One of the things I enjoyed most about the North End was receiving disturbance calls regarding incidents on neighborhood corners or at playgrounds where the local kids had the reputation of being very boisterous loudmouths. They had their own style and they often reminded me of myself growing up in Roxbury. Like most neighborhoods, the North End had its share of troublemakers and druggies. But we knew who they were and I like to think I spoke their language and, by the same token, that they knew I was there to help if they needed it.

The North End certainly spoke its own language. Amazingly, people there could have a complete conversation without saying a word and they had a knack for taking care of business on their own. Traditionally, they didn't trust too many people. But once trust was established they accepted you as one of their own. Once accepted, you became like a part of their family. They had their own code of ethics in the North End and not surprisingly their own agenda, too. They did what they had to do. If it was not the right thing and they got caught, it was their own fault. For the most part, they knew right from wrong. And they knew the score: mess up, get caught, you're gone.

The easiest way to get along with the North End was to sit down and *mangia* (eat). I can remember like it was yesterday the way certain restaurants in the Hanover Street area were the favorite of both cops and the local *cosa nostra*. Giro's on Hanover Street at Commercial, a half block from the Nite Lite Café, was a favorite of many law enforcement officers and a mini-headquarters for wiseguys, but no one did anything there but eat.

Al's on Hanover Street was a favorite to all. I can remember when DA Garrett Byrne asked me to drive him there, I thought, "Oh my God, I know this is a bookie joint." We walked in and everyone acknowledged him, as two games of Gin Rummy continued but all other action stopped—at least for the moment. We had a meal that I will never, ever forget. The food was just delicious—dishes only a true Italian mother could have prepared. Unfortunately, Al's closed and was demolished to make room for a condominium complex.

ECHOES OF GANGLAND

The North End is full of memories for me. I remember one day, standing at roll call waiting for my assignment, when an eerie event occurred. Officer Mike Flemmi, brother of the notorious Stevie "the Rifleman," was there and next to him was Officer Randy La Matinna, son of the notorious "Ralphie Chong" La Matinna. Behind them was Officer Gary Bratsos, whose brother had been murdered by Randy's father. You could cut the tension in the air with a knife.

All of a sudden, Officer La Matinna yelled out to Bratsos, "Stop staring!"

All the TPF men knew the connection between these men, but were unsure of what role, if any, Stevie had played in the murder. These three cops were all dedicated police officers with great records and all three are great friends of mine. But the gangland connections between their families continued to haunt them.

SLOWING DOWN

In the mid 1990s, I was closing in on sixty years of age and on thirty years of motorcycle duty. I never thought of my age much, but as time went by I couldn't help notice the calls of "Hey old-timer, how ya doin'?" Walking in and out of the station house, other officers would joke, "Hey, when you gonna quit and give a young kid a break?" At first it didn't bother me but eventually I realized it was time to think about retiring—or at least slowing down a bit.

I started to look back on the beginning of my career. I went from the Tactical Patrol Force to the District Attorney's Office task force, then on to the Mobile Operations Squad followed by Special Operations and was a member of the elite SWAT team for twenty years. I begin to think that I might be pushing my luck. What I did then was promise myself that I would relax, stay out of trouble and slow down for a couple of years.

During the last five years of my career, Captain Bernard "Bernie" O'Rourke (a sharp, level-headed boss) assigned me to the Downtown Crossing to create a police presence in the area in an attempt to prevent holdups. I would stay there until maybe seven thirty and then head down to the North End. I was to keep Hanover Street clear and to patrol the small streets and alleys, while backing up the sector car.

Not a bad assignment at all. I spent my shifts making friends, talking to the merchants and fielding their complaints. Occasionally a cruiser would drive by, stop and the officer would ask, "Frankie, who do you know to get an assignment like that?"

At seven thirty I would go down to the North End and straight to Modern Pastry for a great cup of coffee and an occasional cannoli. I would sit with the owners Giovanni and Pina and we would talk and enjoy each other's company. At least three times a week Marie Salvati, along with her girlfriend Marie, would join us. Inevitably the conversation would turn to her husband Joe "the Horse" and how he was doing. He was one of many men who had been wrongfully convicted of murder due to Barboza's testimony of lies and he spent time in jail while she raised their children alone. Marie would always say Joe was doing fine, and would talk about the people who had believed in him and cleared his name. "How can I ever repay them?" she'd ask. Whenever the name Joe Barboza came up, a look of great disdain would come over Marie's face. It was obvious that deep down inside Marie was holding a lot of hurt.

I met Joe "the Horse" after he was released from thirty years in prison. For years his lawyer tried to convince the court to review his case, but it wasn't until a local TV reporter, Dan Reye, investigated and helped find out the truth of his innocence that Joe was exonerated. Meeting Joe, I often wondered how he could not hate what I represented.

At about eight thirty or so, I'd sit on my bike and watch the traffic go by and say hi to all the residents of the North End. Almost nightly Joe "the Horse" would come out of his favorite restaurant, Bricco's, to say hello. Joe always talked like one of the boys but when the conversation turned to his wife and kids or grandkids tears would fill his eyes at all the time he lost.

5 North Square Restaurant.

When we finished talking we would always hug and he'd say, "Be careful Frankie."

When the weather turned bad, the merchants would yell for me to come inside and get warm. Such was the case with my good friend George D'Amelio, owner of a restaurant called No. 5 North Square. I had known George and his wife, Lillian, since the mid-sixties, beginning with my time in the DA's office. George had an uncle Fiore who was murdered in a parking lot as he was walking to his car less than four blocks from his home. I can see George's grandfather's face with tears pouring down, begging for us to find his son's killer. It was pretty well-known, and George knew it, that Fiore was getting into trouble and he was warned about it. But Fiore was stubborn.

Lillian had a brother named Al Orlandino, who was a Boston police officer and occasionally rode the bike with me. George had another brother, Christy, who was a cook and a heavy gambler and was unable to work for a living. Christy took one in the head, adding more hurt to the family. George was left with the property so he started a successful restaurant business. We were, and still are, good friends.

In the cold of the winter No. 5 North Square would be my dugout when nothing was going on in the street. I would sit with George while some of our friends stopped by. Tony DeMarco, the former welterweight champion of the world would sit at our table along with one of his handlers and long time friends, Fernando, who was a seafood buyer (especially lobster and crabs). From time to time George would throw a bunch of lobsters and crabs in the pot. While we waited for them to cook, we sat and played all sorts of trivia, from sports to the *Godfather* movies. Our table was even nicknamed "the Goodfellas" table.

In the trivia game it was amazing to see just how knowledgeable Tony was in sports. Tony could remember fighter's names from the time of John L. Sullivan to the present and Tony would tell the story of how he got discovered.

BACK AT "THE GOODFELLAS" TABLE

As Tony and George and I were sitting at our "Goodfellas" table, Tony and George started yelling at me in their North End dialect, trying to convince me to "take care of my own life and get out of this business" so I could live to babysit for my grandkids. They reminded me that I had been boasting about this to all my friends, saying, "I want to be babysitting for my grandkids one of these days."

Tony and George were quick to remind me of Deputy Superintendent Edward Connolly, who, in the twilight of his career, after thirty-eight years on the job, was shot trying to talk a psychopath (someone he had dealt with in the past) into giving himself up after taking his family hostage.

On July 25, 1979, I was patrolling the North End when all of a sudden a SWAT cruiser pulled up and the officer told me to get in the car. He told me that an officer had been shot and was in critical condition at the Faulkner Hospital. While speeding down to 3149 Washington Street in Jamaica Plain, he clued me in on what had happened.

A man had taken his family hostage after Boston Police had surrounded their three-level home. His name was David Sundstrom, a custodian who got into a heated argument with his boss while working in a Boston municipal building. During the outburst, the boss observed a handgun on Sundstrom's waist belt. The boss backed off and proceeded to call the Boston Police. When the custodian arrived at his Washington Street residence, he went into a psychopathic rage, pushing his wife down to the floor. Somehow she managed to call the police who were already at the residence, having been tipped off by his boss. He had taken his wife hostage, along with his mother and four kids ranging in age from thirteen to nine.

It was a hot, sticky night in July and police negotiators from different angles tried to convince Sundstrom to give himself up. Meanwhile, Boston Police got the rundown: Sundstrom was an ex-con who had been busted many times by Connolly or Connolly's men, so Sundstrom was well-known by Connolly. When Connolly arrived at the location, he saw that the house was surrounded by members of the SWAT team and he learned that shots had been fired out of a window. Hundreds of citizens were there to watch what was going on.

Deputy Connolly, now with over thirty-nine years on the job, told the bosses that he knew Sundstrom and thought he could talk him into surrendering. Connolly then went up the five stairs leading to the foyer and began calling for the suspect to give himself up. Meanwhile, my SWAT team positioned ourselves in strategic spots so we could take Sundstrom out if need be. I remember the first position I had was behind a car. As Connolly entered the foyer calling for Sundstrom to come talk to his "friend," a shot rang out and Connolly went down. The suspect ran back into his home and yelled out that he would never give up. Police rushed to the aid of Deputy Connolly and took him to Faulkner Hospital, where he clung to life after being hit with a .45 caliber slug.

The incident began at about 3:15 p.m. It was after 8:15 p.m. when our SWAT team was about to rush the building. At that moment, out came Sundstrom, hiding behind his family and using them as a shield.

5 North Square restaurant; Me, Geri, former assistant trainer Fernando Cardone, former boxer Tony DeMarco and restaurant owners, Lillian and George D'Amelio, waiting on "the Goodfellas" table.

Connolly survived getting shot, but lived only a few more years after that and was in pain until the day he died.

I looked at George and then at Tony and I said to them, "Okay boys, let's play trivia. Enough is enough. It's time for me to stop and play with those grandkids. It is time to end my career."

19.

End of the Ride

Changing Times

One of the most incredible things I've found in my career is the way in which the make-up of the department has changed. In March of 1964 my academy class consisted of forty-four Boston police recruits and five recruits from the Brookline Police Department. They were all white males with the exception of one of Boston's finest. His name was Paul and I can remember the "friendly" abuse he would take. We kept asking him where he was from and he would say he was from Boston and that he was half Spanish. We all knew he was uncomfortable at first, but as time went by the class became very tight.

Throughout your career, occasionally you'll bump into an old classmate and the closeness you feel toward each other is remarkable. We could relate to all the uncomfortable assignments we got at the academy. We could recall all the good times and the bad times, while always keeping tabs on each other's progress in the department. Conversations among brother officers would always include how many bosses came out of their class and others would state how many weirdos they had in theirs. The camaraderie among classmates for the most part was intense. Everyone would watch the progress of each other's career and would ask, "How's he doing?"

Comparing the make-up of the recruits of the sixties to that of the present time is mind-boggling. In order to serve and communicate with such a diverse population, departments must hire more minority personnel to better serve the entire community. Present recruits learn the basics as well as "community policing" and everything they do includes the use of computers. Not only are the classes very diverse, but they are much larger—

sometimes over one hundred in a class. And cadets train in the academy for more than six months.

Well, there I was, thirty-nine and a half years later thinking back on that cold March day in 1964 when I graduated from the academy and remembering how thrilled and proud I was to be joining the best police department in the country (which I truly believe to this day). I was also thinking of all my brother and sister officers who I met and worked with throughout the years. I will never forget the courage and bravery I observed through the duration of my career.

At the end of my ride, all I had to do was stay out of trouble, remain a high-profile presence and be nice to the citizens, while staying available to the owners and operators of the businesses in the Downtown Crossing and the North End.

INCIDENT IN DOWNTOWN CROSSING

After some time, the Downtown Crossing area became more and more difficult as gang members, along with junkies from the outskirts of the city, began pushing there. Complaints started coming in from merchants and more and more potential customers were feeling unsafe in the area. As a result, many people started shopping in the malls. It seemed that the world was changing right in front of me and I couldn't do anything about it. The more aggressive I got, the more complaints the bosses would get about me, most saying I was harassing the young citizenry.

I thought I had seen it all with nearly forty years on the job when about a week before my retirement I was confronted by a hysterical young woman who reported that a priest was being pistol-whipped by a man in front of Saint Anthony's Shrine on Arch Street. Through the years I have become accustomed, as has any other officer with any number of years on the job, to calls similar to this. But I was worried that day that my luck would run out. Before approaching the location, I called the dispatcher to alert him to the situation. I asked for a backup and requested that no sirens be used by cruisers responding to my call. As I approached the site, people were running toward me and yelling that there was a man with a gun beating a priest. Sure enough, there stood the man, his left hand holding the priest by the throat and in plain view I could see a gun in his right hand. With my weapon in my hand I approached the man and told him to drop his gun. With this, he turned in my direction, gun still in hand. At that moment my backup arrived—the suspect didn't see or hear them coming—and they disarmed and arrested him.

I later thought how horrible it would have been to leave the job had I needed to use my service weapon. The arrest was given to the young backup officers who were thrilled to get it. Years ago, that would be my "pinch," but the thought of booking him and filing the report by computer turned me off.

Once the suspect was processed, I headed to the North End, straight to No. 5 North Square, where I met up with Tony and George. After telling them what had just happened, George looked at me and said, "Are you crazy?"

Tony turned and asked, "Why don't you go home and write a book like I'm doing?"

I knew that there had been many books written detailing the events of the 1960s and most are generally true. What I had experienced was a career full of excitement, fun and the unknown. These were all things I could handle, things that I expected. All those years on the street I was the boss, in command and knew the chain of command.

My career ended with a great surprise party at City Hall Plaza thrown by the mayor, Police Commissioner Paul Evans and co-coordinated by Special Events Director Patti Pappa. My family was also there, to my surprise. There were hundreds of officers, superintendents, motorcycle officers and even police cadets. At that time I was wearing Badge #1 for being the most senior officer in the department. When I left, I felt fulfilled in what I had accomplished.

FINAL WORD

Summing up all of my experiences—both good and bad—and sharing them with so many people, I feel honored to have been part of such a great police department. Within most departments, police officers graduate from their academies after a long, tedious and very stressful amount of time, sometimes as much as six months. Without a doubt police officers receive the best training their city can give and graduate more than ready for just about anything. They are prepared physically and intellectually, with all of the resources available: computers, better weapons, communications, etc. But what they need most and what can't be taught is common sense.

In my rookie year of 1964, I remember hitting the street after three months in the academy. For me, common sense came from listening to the veteran officers with whom I rode. I kept my mouth shut while I observed them and learned.

Pinning Badge #1 on the new recipient, Bob Guiney.

Protocol is only a word now, but I can remember in my early days entering my first assigned precinct, District 13, and saluting the front desk even though the seat was empty.

About the Author

Frankie D. was born and raised in the city of Boston where he still lives to this day with his wife, Geri.

After retirement from the Boston Police Department, Frankie DeSario was hired by the Boston Red Sox and has been with them for the past three seasons, including their championship and World Series victory.

Bob Bandera and me at Fenway Park.

Former Red Sox's All-Star Pitcher Luis Tiant and me.

Please visit us at
www.historypress.net